A CREATIVE GUIDE TO

KNITTED LACE

JAN EATON

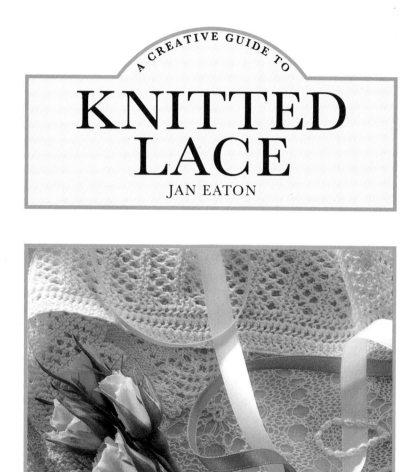

NH
NEW
HOLLAND

First published in 1994 by
New Holland (Publishers) Ltd
London • Cape Town • Sydney • Singapore

Reprinted 1996

24 Nutford Place
London W1H 6DQ
United Kingdom

80 McKenzie Street
Cape Town 8001
South Africa

3/2 Aquatic Drive
Frenchs Forest, NSW 2086
Australia

ISBN 1 85368 290 X

Editor Coral Walker
Assistant editor Sue Thraves
Art director Jane Forster
Photographer Steve Tanner
Illustrators Stephen Dew and Coral Mula

The author would like to thank the following:
Janet Bentley for her invaluable work writing and charting
patterns from historical pieces of knitted lace
Annette Claxton and Jane Easson-Brown for their help and
encouragement
DMC Creative World for supplying sample threads
Framecraft for supplying the crystal jar on page 38

Typeset by Ace Filmsetting Ltd, Frome, Somerset
Reproduction by Scantrans Pte Ltd, Singapore
Printed and bound in Malaysia by Times Offset (M) SDN BHD.

The craft of knitting

Knitting dates back to the seventh century and has a long and distinguished history. From the patterned table carpets of the European knitting guilds to fine Elizabethan stockings and the wonderfully intricate shawls still made in the Shetland Isles, knitting skills have spread throughout much of the world. In recent times, knitting has been one of the most popular pastimes for both women and men, with a wealth of yarns and patterns available to whet even the most jaded appetite.

Many people knit sweaters, scarves and baby clothes, but few modern knitters are familiar with the beauty of lace made in this way. Whether worked in rows or rounds, a piece of knitted lace can be as fine, light and delicate as a cobweb or thick and soft with an interesting texture. The difference depends not only on the stitch pattern being used, but also on your choice of yarn and needles.

A LOOK BACK IN TIME

Knitting is the craft of making a looped fabric from a continuous length of yarn using two or more eyeless needles. The fabric can be flat or tubular. The craft has a long history with the earliest known pieces – discovered in parts of the Middle East – dating back to the seventh century. Textile fragments excavated from earlier cultures, Peruvian (900 BC to AD 600) and Coptic (4th century AD), were thought to show examples of knitting, but extensive studies of the fabrics have shown that the fragments were not constructed from one continuous piece of yarn. Instead, separate lengths were used, looped together using a needle with an eye.

The fragments of knitting which date from the seventh century show evidence of great skill and technical proficiency on the part of the workers – the pieces are knitted with coloured yarn in sophisticated geometric patterns which reflect contemporary tile and carpet designs. Although there is no hard evidence to allow us to trace the spread of knitting accurately from these early beginnings, it is safe to assume that knitting was brought by traders, sailors and soldiers from the Middle East to Europe.

The earliest reference to knitting in Europe is in a fourteenth century painting by Master Bertram. The painting, called 'The Visit of Angels', is part of the Buxtehude altarpiece and shows the Virgin Mary picking up stitches on a knitted shirt using four double-pointed needles. The name 'knitting' is taken from the Anglo-Saxon word *cnittan*, meaning threads woven by hand.

By the mid sixteenth century, the craft of knitting had spread widely throughout Europe and the first knitting guild was formed in Paris in 1527. Guilds were almost exclusively a male preserve – women had the tedious task of spinning the yarn, then it was knitted up by men, a much more skilled and therefore prestigious occupation. Widows were the only women allowed to enter guild membership, providing their husband had been a guild member and they could cope with their dead husband's entire workload themselves. Guilds promoted a very high standard of craftsmanship with apprentices having to work and study for six years before knitting and preparing a shirt, a pair of socks, a felted cap and a colourwork carpet for their final examination.

As knitting guilds spread through Europe, different countries became renowned for making particular types of garments. France, Spain and Italy produced delicate, lacy silk gloves, stockings and jackets, while in southern Europe most knitting was worked into church vestments and ornaments. By contrast, in Germany and Austria, the majority of knitting was worked in wool yarn and the knitted fabric was usually heavily embroidered. This region became famous for making large knitted table carpets which were also used as luxurious wall hangings. The carpets were worked on a knitting frame instead of needles. The frames were set with pegs round which various colours of yarn were wound to make loops. The loops were then slipped off the pegs to create a knitted fabric. Although this technique had virtually died out by the mid nineteenth century, it still survives today in the form of the colourful tubes of bobbin or 'French' knitting made by children.

In England, knitted stockings became fashionable after Queen Elizabeth I accepted a pair of knitted silk stockings as a New Year's gift in 1560. This period heralded the beginning of knitting as both a flourishing domestic handicraft and a cottage industry, particularly as wool production was an important part of the country's economy.

EARLY KNITTING NEEDLES

The earliest knitting needles were made from a variety of materials including wood, copper, bone, metal wire, ivory and tortoiseshell and they became prized possessions. Needles were referred to by various terms during the sixteenth century, frequently they were called 'wires' or 'pins', particularly in Essex. The inventory of a Durham mercer, John Farbeck, dated 20 November 1597 refers to them as 'knitting pricks'; while an Italian dictionary compiled and published by John Florio in 1598 gives the first recorded mention of 'knitting needles'.

Needles were often made by the knitters themselves. The points were kept sharp by regularly regrinding and they were carefully protected with wooden or cork stoppers. When not in use, knitting needles were wrapped in leather folders or stored in cases or carved wood or ivory.

Knitting sheaths or sticks were used to speed up the work – essential for those knitting for a living. The sheaths, often beautifully carved and decorated, were tucked into the knitter's belt or apron strings on the right hip. The sheath held the end of the right-hand needle firmly, leaving the right hand free to knit, moving the stitches rapidly from needle to needle. As many as 200 stitches a minute could be knitted in this way by a skilled worker. Knitting sheaths were often made by young men for their sweethearts, carved with intertwined initials, hearts, flowers and even mottoes.

By the mid sixteenth century, knitting had become accepted as an important method of making fabric. A law of 1565 ruled that every person older than seven years had to wear, on pain of a fine, 'upon the Sabbath or holyday upon their head a cap of wool knitted, thickened and dressed in England'. Many of these knitted and felted woollen caps still exist in museums throughout the country. The caps were knitted, then the fabric was thickened by immersion in water for several days so the wool fibres felted together to make a solid mat. The cap was shaped and dried on a wooden block, then the surface was brushed into a pile with a teasel brush. This process resulted in a thick, warm fabric which could even be cut without the yarn unravelling. Today, the traditional French beret and Turkish fez are still made in the same way.

Towards the close of the sixteenth century, demand for knitted garments, particularly stockings for both men and women, began to outstrip production. William Lee, a graduate from Cambridge University, invented a rudimentary knitting machine between 1589 and 1600. Lee was unsuccessful in promoting his machine, which made stockings on a frame, mainly because its use was seen as a potential threat to the livelihood of handknitters. Gradually, however, the use of frames was developed. Although the Framework Knitters' Guild was granted a charter of incorporation as early as July 1657 and the days of commercial knitting by hand were in reality numbered, the development of mechanised knitting was very slow and hand knitting continued to flourish as a cottage industry for another 200 years.

Many knitted pieces survive from the seventeenth century, usually in the form of ecclesiastical vestments or ornate garments made for court wear for the aristocracy, and these include beautifully patterned altar gloves knitted in red silks and gold threads and the Italian silk undershirt worn by King Charles I at his execution in 1649.

KNITTING FOR LEISURE

As hand knitting gradually declined commercially, so the craft went through a revival as a purely domestic occupation. By the nineteenth century, the growth of a leisured class of women meant that much more time could be spent on working fine needlecrafts, particularly knitting, crochet and embroidery.

Intricate lace knitting worked in fine yarn on very fine needles became popular and many new lace stitches and patterns were invented during this period and used to make mittens, bonnets, shawls, tablecloths and layettes. Tiny glass and cut steel beads were threaded on to fine cotton or linen yarn and worked into intricately patterned purses and pincushions. Ladies' journals and magazines published knitting stitches and patterns regularly, but in the more remote communities it was still the tradition to pass on patterns by word of mouth from generation to generation.

The traditional colourwork patterns worked by knitters from the Fair Isles, for example, are reputed to have originated from Spanish sailors swept ashore after the ill-fated expedition of the Spanish Armada in 1588 when many of the defeated ships were wrecked by storms. The majority of Fair Isle patterns have survived unchanged throughout the centuries and are still worked from memory rather than from written instructions. Patterns for Shetland shawls, beautiful lacy creations so fine that some can be passed through a wedding ring without harm, are handed down in the same way.

Knitting has remained one of the most popular pastimes during this century, probably reaching a peak in the 1930s and 1940s when the hand-knitted 'woollie' was in fashion.

Machine-made steel, and later aluminium and plastic, needles were inexpensive and readily available together with machine-spun and chemically dyed yarns. Magazines continued to publish a wide range of stitches and patterns, and there have been many excellent books published on the subject including Mary Thomas's books on stitches (*Book of Knitting Patterns*, 1943) and techniques (*Knitting Book*, 1938) and, more recently, Montse Stanley's *Handknitters' Handbook* (1986).

The more elaborate knitted lace pieces in this book, including the raised leaf Victorian bedspread (page 136) and the circular tablecloth (page 125), are from my collection of antique linen dating from the 1880s to the 1920s. My maternal grandmother, an expert knitter, used a raised leaf design similar to the bedspread motif when she knitted a colourful blanket for me during the early 1960s from her yarn oddments. I still treasure the blanket nearly thirty years later and, in spite of the occasional repair to a seam, the knitting is still going strong.

Specific yarns, hook sizes and tension have not been quoted for these designs, but the patterns have been written and charted for you to recreate these fine pieces of knitting and make heirlooms for your own family. A needle size/yarn thickness chart is given below to help you select the appropriate materials.

The remaining projects have been designed specially for this book, particularly with beginners in mind. The crystal bath salts jar on page 38 makes the ideal introduction to knitted lace, while the edging round the scented sachets (page 32) give the beginner useful practice at working an edging with points. Each project is graded with a degree-of-difficulty symbol so you can tell at a glance which projects are suitable for your level of experience and ability.

The pattern library on pages 64 to 77 contains over 30 more stitch patterns for knitted lace including eyelet and large-scale lace patterns for shawls and wraps, a border, motif and insertion featuring raised leaf designs, plus a selection of edgings, borders and insertions for decorating all items of household linen in various sizes, from towels to pillowcases.

NOTE FOR LEFT-HANDED READERS
When following the diagrams for working knitting stitches and techniques, prop the book up in front of a large mirror so the diagrams are reflected in reverse (ie left-handed) form.

NOTES FOR NORTH AMERICAN READERS
Both metric and imperial measurements are used throughout the book and there is a needle conversion chart on page 12. However, there are a few differences in knitting terminology and yarn names which are given below:

UK terms	US terms
Cast off	Bind off
Stocking stitch	Stockinette
Work straight	Work even
Tension	Gauge

UK yarn names	US yarn names
3 ply	Lightweight
4 ply	Fingering or mediumweight
Double knitting	Sport
Aran weight	Worsted or fisherman
Double-double or chunky	Heavyweight or bulky

Chart for knitted lace yarn weight/ needle size combinations

Fine crochet cottons	1¼ mm–2¾ mm
2 ply	2¼ mm–3 mm
3 ply	2¾ mm–3¾ mm
4 ply	3 mm–4 mm
Double knitting	3¾ mm–4½ mm
Aran	4½ mm–5½ mm
Chunky	5½ mm–7½ mm

Practical Skills

There is a wide variety of yarns available which can be used to make knitted lace. Traditionally, this was worked in very fine cotton, linen or wool yarns but today almost any type of yarn with a smooth surface is acceptable. The weight of yarns you can use for working knitted lace varies from the finest mercerized cotton to double knitting weight wool. However, hairy yarns such as mohair and textured, knobbly yarns are not successful; a lace stitch pattern worked in mohair will be indistinct while a pattern worked in textured yarn will pull out of shape.

Yarn for knitting is usually sold ready-wound into balls of a specific size and the amount contained in each ball is quoted by weight rather than by length. The weight is given in grams or ounces – the most common ball sizes are 25 g or 50 g (1 oz or 2 oz) – and the length of yarn in the ball will vary from yarn to yarn depending on thickness. Occasionally, yarn is sold in coiled hanks or skeins and this must be wound by hand into balls before you start knitting. Fine cotton yarn is sold in a small, flattened ball wound round card or plastic and this type of yarn is usually labelled with length as well as weight.

Pure wool and wool/synthetic mixtures are formed by twisting together a number of strands or 'plies'. The finished yarns are available in several weights, from fine 2 ply to heavy, double-double knitting weight (also known as chunky). You can obtain a very fine Shetland wool, 1ply, spun specially for knitting traditional lacy Shetland shawls, but this is usually available only by mail order from spinners based in the Shetland Isles. Use the quoted ply as a general guide to the thickness of the yarn, as yarn measurements are not standard from spinner to spinner and the thickness will vary according to the degree of twist.

Thick cotton yarns are also available in 2-plies, 4-ply and double knitting. Many of the finer cotton yarns available in the shops are labelled as crochet cotton, and are particularly good for working knitted lace as these yarns are mercerized, making them smooth and very strong with a slightly glossy surface. The thickness of crochet yarns is graded by a series of numbers, from the coarsest (No 3) to the finest (No 60). In some countries very fine thread indeed, up to No 100, is available.

For the beginner, double-knitting weight wool or a wool/synthetic mixture is ideal for practising stitches, patterns and techniques. Wool retains a certain amount of

stretch and 'give' when it is spun into a yarn and this makes stitches easier to work. Begin by using a 4 mm knitting needles. When you have become familiar with using the wool yarn, change to a smooth cotton yarn of about the same thickness and work your stitches in this, again using a 4 mm needles. Cotton yarn is harder on the fingers than wool and has very little 'give' in it, but lace stitch patterns show up well. When you feel confident handling this weight of yarn and size of needles, move on to finer yarns and needles. The chart on page 9 gives information about needle sizes and suggests yarn weight/needle size combinations.

BALL BAND INFORMATION

Each ball of knitting yarn is wrapped in a paper band (called a ball band) which gives you lots of useful information about the yarn. As well as fibre composition and the weight of the ball, it will also show the colour and dye lot number, symbols for washing and pressing instructions and often a range of suitable needle sizes plus tension details. International yarn care symbols are shown below.

The dye lot number on the ball band is particularly important as when the yarn is dyed in batches there are often subtle variations in colour between lots. Although this difference may not be apparent when you compare balls of yarn in your hand, it will probably show as a shade variation when the yarn is knitted and may look unsightly. Always use yarn from the same dye lot for a single project.

Make sure you keep a ball band for each piece of knitted lace you work. Keep it in a small, polythene 'grip-top' bag with any left-over yarn and label the bag with details of the item you have made. You will then be able to refer to the washing instructions and have the correct yarn ready to make any necessary repairs.

NEILES AND OTHER EQUIPMENT

Knitting needles

Modern knitting needles are made from coated aluminium, plastic, bamboo or wood and all of them are light and easy to work with. Choice is really a matter of preference – some knitters prefer aluminium needles as they bend less easily than other types, while others choose plastic or bamboo as they are silent in use

Type of care	Dry cleaning	Washing	Bleaching	Drying	Ironing
Fairly easy care	(A) Use any dry-cleaning fluid	6/40° Machine-wash at stated temperature	△Cl Chlorine (household) bleach may be used	◯ Can be tumble dried	High setting – hot
Treat carefully	(P) Use perchlorethylene or white spirit only	30° Hand wash at stated temperature		▢ Dry on a line	Medium setting – warm
Handle with great care	(F) Use white spirit only	Wash by hand only		▦ Allow to drip dry	Low setting – cool
Do not use treatment shown	⊗ Must not be dry-cleaned	Must not be washed	Do not use household bleach	▭ Do not hang – lay flat	Must not be ironed

and do not 'click'. Needles for flat knitting are sold in pairs and are pointed at one end for easy stitch formation and have a knob at the other end to keep the stitches in place. They are sold in three different lengths, 25 cm, 30 cm and 35 cm (10 in, 12 in and 14 in) – so choose the right length for the job in hand. For example, use short needles when edging and long ones when knitting a lace wrap or large bedspread square. Each needle is marked with its size either at the top of the shaft or, alternatively, on the knob.

The most common knitting needles range in size from fine 2mm needles to chunky 10 mm ones, although some European needle manufacturers offer a wider range of sizes, from 1½ mm right up to 17 mm. The size of the needle is measured around the body of the shaft and all modern British and European needles are sold in metric sizes. The chart below gives a list of metric sizes, together with numbers from the previous British numerical system and gives details of the American equivalents.

Needle Conversion Chart

USA	UK	Metric
0	14	2
1	13	2¼
		2½
2	12	2¾
	11	3
3	10	3¼
4		3½
5	9	3¾
6	8	4
7	7	4½
8	6	5
9	5	5½
10	4	6
10½	3	6½
	2	7
	1	7½
11	0	8
13	00	9
15	000	10

Double-pointed needles
Double-pointed needles are used when knitting in the round (see the circular tea cloth on page 47) and they are sold in sets of four or six. Double-pointed needles are available in a similar range of sizes to ordinary knitting needles, but individual needles are not marked with the size.

Circular needles
Circular needles are used to work a circular piece of knitting without a seam. They are often used in preference to sets of double-pointed needles (above) when a large number of stitches is being worked (see circular tea cloth, page 47). A circular needle consists of two needle ends permanently linked by a supple piece of thin nylon cord. They are available in the same needle sizes as double-pointed needles, but also in different cord lengths. Choose a cord length to suit the number of stitches you are working, making sure that your knitting fits on the needle without stretching out of shape. Substitute increasingly longer needles as the number of stitches grows. It is quite easy to remove any kinks from the nylon cord by dipping it in a bowl of very hot water.

Needle gauge
This is a shaped piece of metal or plastic punched with holes corresponding to needle sizes. The holes are marked with both modern metric sizes and the old numerical system. To check the size of a needle, simply slot it into the closest hole and read off the size. This is a particularly useful gadget when using double-pointed needles as they are not marked with the size.

Row counter
An invaluable piece of equipment, the row counter is a short cylinder with a numbered dial which is slipped on to one

needle close to the knob. The dial is turned at the end of every row.

Markers

Split loops made from brightly coloured plastic which can be clipped on to a stitch to mark a place in the knitting. These are especially useful to mark the end of rounds in circular knitting. Short lengths of coloured yarn can be tied to a stitch instead to mark a place.

Tapestry needles

Tapestry (also called yarn) needles have long eyes and blunt points. Keep a selection of sizes handy and use them when finishing thread ends and for sewing pieces of knitting together. Use ordinary sewing needles when applying a knitted edging, border or insertion to a piece of fabric.

Other equipment

Keep a bag or workbox handy containing general sewing equipment including sharp scissors, stainless steel pins with glass or plastic heads, a good quality dressmakers' tape measure, sewing needles and threads. Large safety pins are useful for securing a dropped stitch while you deal with it and a small crochet hook makes a useful tool for picking up dropped stitches.

CALCULATING YOUR REQUIREMENTS

As many of the knitted lace projects in this book were made in the early part of this century, the yarns used cannot be identified and are probably no longer available, so reliable guidelines to yarn quantities cannot be given. The smaller projects, for example the crystal jar cover (page 38) and lace-edged handkerchief (page 37), require less than 1 ball of yarn.

For the larger projects such as the evening wrap on page 30, the best way to calculate your yarn requirement is to knit up one complete ball of your chosen yarn

in the pattern you wish to work, after first knitting samples to check the compatibility of yarn and needles. Cast off at the end of the ball, pin out and block (page 24) your piece and allow it to dry. Next, look to see how many pattern repeats could be knitted from one ball of yarn and divide this figure into the total number of repeats you need. For example, if one ball of yarn makes four repeats of the pattern and you would like 32 repeats in total, you will need to buy eight balls of yarn, plus extra for the fringes. Always buy slightly more yarn than you think you will need – odd balls can always be used up or whole balls of surplus yarn may sometimes be returned for a refund. Check before purchase.

TENSION

When working a piece of knitting you must make sure that the fabric you produce is neither too loose and floppy nor too tightly knitted and stiff. It is also important that the needle size you have selected is compatible with the weight of yarn you are using. This is called tension (also known as gauge) and is usually quoted as a number of rows and stitches over a given area of knitted fabric, usually 10 cm (4 in) square. When knitting a garment, correct tension is vital to ensure that the garment is the correct size when finished. Garment patterns include a tension guideline stating the number of rows and stitches which must be achieved. With items of home furnishing, the size is less crucial and the effect and handling quality of the finished knitted fabric is more important.

Because many different yarn weights can be used to make the projects in the book, specific yarns, needle sizes and tension cannot be quoted with any accuracy. The pattern instructions suggest a type of yarn, for example double knitting weight cotton, but you could substitute a finer yarn if you prefer. Apply common sense when choosing yarn for a project – obviously a dainty handkerchief edging would be far too clumsy knitted in thick yarn, while a bedspread would be equally impractical knitted in fine yarn on large needles as it would not keep its shape. The chart on page 9 suggests various needle size and yarn weight combinations and remember also that many yarns give a range of suitable needle sizes on the ball band.

Instead of working to a specific stitch and row count when knitting the projects, make several small sample pieces with your chosen yarn and needles to check the results you will get before beginning to work the real thing. Knitted lace should be light and holey, but the knitted fabric should not be so loose that the stitches will pull out of shape when the article is handled. Remember that tension is a very individual thing – two knitters using exactly the same pattern, yarn and needles will always produce slightly different results. As a general rule, if your samples are too tight and stiff, change to a larger size of needle, while if the fabric is too loose and floppy, use a smaller size needle.

CASTING ON

Thumb method

This method uses one needle and the left thumb and results in a soft, elastic edge. Make sure you allow sufficient yarn to make all the cast-on stitches.

1 Make a slip knot about 1 m (1 yd) or more from the end of the yarn and place it on the needle. Hold the needle and the loose end of yarn in your right hand and wind the yarn from the ball over your left thumb to make a loop as shown.

2 Insert the needle into the loop, wind the loose end of yarn over the needle point.

3 Pull a loop through to form the stitch and tighten the loose end to secure the stitch. Repeat to cast on all the stitches.

Finger method
The second method uses one needle and the index finger of the left hand. It makes a loose, lacy edge, but you must take care when working the first row as the cast-on stitches can easily spring off the needle.

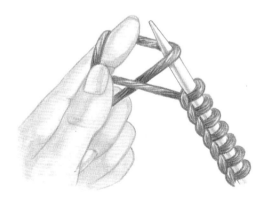

1 Make a slip knot about 10 cm (4 in) from the end of the yarn and place it on the needle. Hold the needle in your right hand.

2 Wind the yarn round your finger to make a loop, as shown, and slip the needle point into the loop. Tighten the loop on the needle and repeat along the row.

STITCHES AND YARN MOVEMENTS
Knit stitch (k)

1 With the yarn at the back of the work, insert the right-hand needle through the first stitch on the left-hand needle from front to back.

2 Wind the yarn over the right-hand needle as shown.

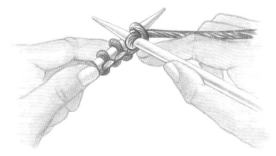

3 Pull a loop of yarn through to make a new stitch on the right-hand needle.

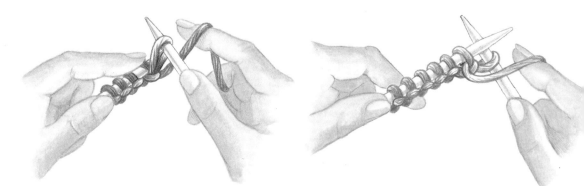

4 Slip the original stitch off the left-hand needle, leaving the new stitch on the right-hand needle. Repeat along the row until all the stitches have been transferred to the right-hand needle.

Purl stitch (p)

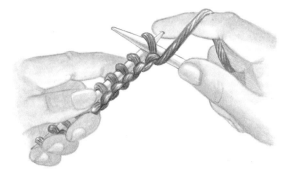

1 With the yarn at the front of the work, insert the right-hand needle through the front of the first in the row of stitches on the left-hand needle.

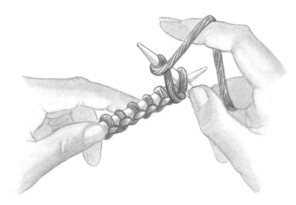

2 Wind the yarn round the right-hand needle as shown.

3 Pull a loop of yarn through to make a new stitch on the right-hand needle.
4 Slip the original stitch off the left-hand needle, leaving the new stitch on the right-hand needle. Repeat along the row until all the stitches have been transferred to the right-hand needle.

Knit two stitches together (k2 tog)

Decrease a stitch by inserting the right-hand needle through the front of the next two stitches on the left-hand needle and knit both stitches together. Work k3 tog in the same way, but knit three stitches instead of two.

Knit two stitches together through the back of the loop (k 2 tog tbl)

Work the same as k2 tog, but insert the right-hand needle through the back instead of the front of the two stitches.

Purl two stitches together (p2 tog)

Purl two stitches together through the back of the loop (p2 tog tbl)

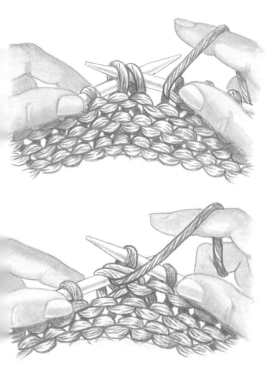

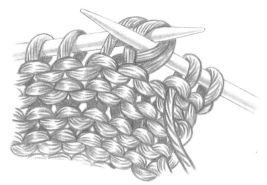

Decrease a stitch by inserting the right-hand needle through the front of the next two stitches on the left-hand needle and purl both stitches together. Work p3 tog in the same way, but purl three stitches instead of two.

Work the same as p2 tog, but insert the right-hand needle through the back instead of the front of the two stitches.

Slip one, knit one, pass slipped stitch over (sl 1, k1, psso)

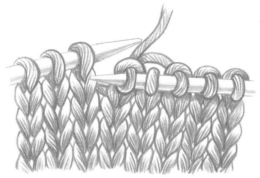

1 Slip the next stitch from the left-hand needle on to the right-hand needle without working it. Knit the next stitch on the left-hand needle in the usual way.

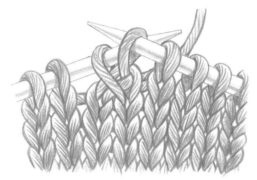

2 Using the left-hand needle point, lift the slipped stitch over the last stitch you have worked and off the right-hand needle to decrease one stitch.

Yarn over (yo)

In knitted lace, holes in the fabric are made by taking the yarn over the needle to make a loop which is worked as a stitch on the following row creating a hole. The yarn movement (the way in which the yarn is taken over the needle) depends on the stitches at either side, whether they are two knit stitches, two purl stitches, a knit and a purl stitch or a purl and a knit stitch. In this book, the abbreviation 'yo' is used for all these yarn movements unless otherwise stated.

Working yo between two knit stitches
Bring the yarn forward to the front of the work between the needles and knit the next stitch in the usual way. The yarn makes an extra loop over the right-hand needle as you do this. Treat this loop as a stitch on the following row.

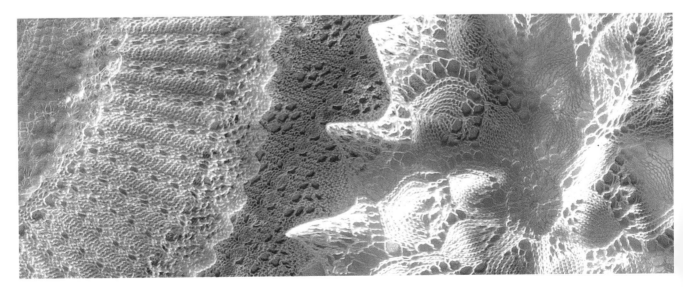

Working yo between two purl stitches
Take the yarn right round the right-hand needle point and bring it out at the front of the work ready to purl the next stitch. Treat the resulting loop as a stitch on the following row.

Working yo between a knit and a purl stitch Bring the yarn forward to the front of the work between the needles. Take the yarn over the right-hand needle and back to the front ready to purl the next stitch. Treat the resulting loop as a stitch on the following row.

Working yo between a purl and a knit stitch After working the purl stitch, the yarn is already at the front of the work. Proceed to knit the next stitch in the usual way. The yarn makes an extra loop over the right-hand needle as you do this. Treat this loop as a stitch on the following row.

Increase (inc)

This can be worked in two ways:
1 Knit the next stitch on the left-hand needle in the usual way, but do not slip the original stitch from the left-hand needle. Knit again into this stitch, inserting the right-hand needle into the back of the stitch, then slip it off the needle. This makes two stitches from the original one.

2 Knit the next stitch on the left-hand needle in the usual way, but do not slip the original stitch from the left-hand needle. Instead, purl into this stitch before slipping it off the needle, making two new stitches from the original one.

Wherever the abbreviation 'inc' appears in this book, look under the special abbreviations section to find which method to use. Make sure you follow the correct instruction for the particular pattern you are using as the effect produced by these two methods looks different.

CASTING OFF

To make a soft, elastic cast-off edge, cast off in the same stitch you are using (ie either knit or purl) and use one or two sizes larger for the right-hand needle.

1 Knit the first two stitches in the usual way so they are both taken over on to the right-hand needle.

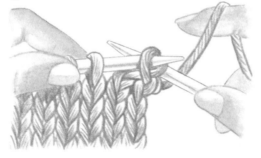

2 Using the left-hand needle point, lift the first stitch over the second stitch and off the needle.

3 Knit the next stitch so there are two stitches again on the right-hand needle and repeat step 2. Continue repeating steps 2 and 3 until there is one stitch remaining on the right-hand needle. Break off the yarn, lengthen the last stitch and pull the cut end through. Pull the yarn to tighten the stitch.

JOINING A NEW BALL OF YARN

Never, join a new ball of yarn in the middle of a row. This will not only look unsightly, but it makes a weak place in the knitting which may unravel in use. Instead, always make sure to join in the new yarn at the end of the row.

1 Knot the new yarn to the first stitch, leaving a long end to fasten off later.

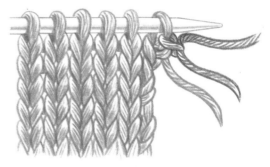

2 Work the first stitch with two yarns – one from the new ball and the end of the old yarn. Drop the old yarn and continue working with the new ball.

DOUBLE-POINTED NEEDLES

Knitting in the round on double-pointed needles can produce lovely circular pieces of knitted lace. When knitting with four needles, three needles hold the stitches in a triangular shape while the fourth (the working needle) is held in the right hand and used to knit the stitches. (The simplest way of thinking about the arrangement is to remember that the three needles holding the stitches represent the left-hand needle in conventional knitting and the fourth or working needle represents the right-hand needle.) When all the stitches from one needle have been worked, then that needle becomes the working needle.

Most circular knitting patterns use four needles, but some may use five or six. In this case, use one needle as the working needle and divide the stitches evenly between the remaining needles.

Although circular knitting may feel very cumbersome at first, it will become easier with practice. As the work is not turned at the end of each row in circular knitting, the right side of the knitting is always facing you. Take care to mark the beginning of each round with a marker.

1 Cast the number of stitches stated in the pattern on to one of the needles. Divide the stitches equally between three needles and tie a loop of contrasting yarn on to the needle and the left-hand end of the

stitches. This loop marks the beginning of new rounds.

2 Arrange the needles in a triangle, taking care not to twist the stitches. Take the fourth needle and slip the marker loop on to it, then insert the needle into the first stitch on the third needle and knit the stitch. Continue knitting until all the stitches have been transferred to the fourth needle and the third needle then becomes the working needle.

Use the working needle to knit the stitches on the second needle then, in turn, use the new working needle to knit the stitches on the first needle to complete the first round. Pull the yarn tightly when changing needles to avoid holes forming and remember to transfer the marker loop at the beginning of every round.

KNITTING ABBREVIATIONS

k	knit	*alt*	alternate
p	purl	*beg*	beginning
st(s)	stitch(es)	*foll*	following
k2 tog	knit two stitches together	*patt*	pattern
p2 tog	purl two stitches together	*tog*	together
tbl	through the back of loop(s)	*RS*	right side
sl	slip	*WS*	wrong side
psso	pass slipped stitch over	* repeat a sequence of stitches from that point	
yo	yarn over needle	[] the sequence inside square brackets must be repeated the given number of times	
rep	repeat		
rem	remaining	() round brackets contain extra information to help you, not instructions	
cont	continue		

HOW TO FOLLOW A WRITTEN PATTERN

Knitting patterns are written in a logical way, even though at first sight the instructions can look rather complicated. The most important thing to remember when following a pattern is to check that you cast on the correct number of stitches and then work through the instructions step by step *exactly* as stated.

Begin by reading the pattern through before you start to knit. As well as instructions, the pattern will contain information about materials, measurements and finishing off the item. Although some instructions or details may not be clear on the first reading, the technique involved will be much easier to grasp once the work is in front of you.

Many knitting abbreviations are standard and found in most patterns. A list of standard abbreviations and their meanings is given on page 21. Any special abbreviations are explained on the relevant pattern.

Asterisks

In order to make written patterns shorter and avoid tedious repetition, asterisks like this * are used to indicate which sections of the instructions have to be repeated across a row.

For example, an instruction such as 'K2, * k1, p4; rep from * to end' means that you begin the row by knitting the first two stitches, then you must work repeats of knit one stitch, purl four stitches right across the row until all the stitches on the left-hand needle have been used up.

Instead of the instruction 'rep from * to end', you may find something like 'rep from * to last 2 sts, k2'. In this case, work complete repeats of the instructions after the asterisk until there are only two stitches remaining on the needle, then you must knit these two stitches.

Square brackets

Square brackets [] fulfil a similar function to asterisks and both may be used in the same pattern row. Always repeat the sequence of stitches shown inside the square brackets for the stated number of times before proceeding to the next instruction in the row. For example, a pattern row reading 'K2, * K2, p4, [sl 1, k1, psso, k2 tog] twice, p4; rep from * to end' instructs you to knit the first two stitches, then work repeats of knit two, purl four, slip one, knit one, pass slipped stitch over, knit two together, slip one, knot one, pass slipped stitch over, knit two together, purl four, until all the stitches on the left-hand needle have been used up.

Round brackets

Round brackets () do not contain working instructions. Instead, they give extra information which the knitter may find helpful, for example the number of stitches which should be on the needle at the end of a particular row.

Repeats

Each stitch pattern is written using a specific number of pattern rows and row sequence must be repeated until the knitting is the correct length. A simple pattern such as the edging for the handkerchief on page 37 is four rows long, for example, while the deep edging on the towel on page 56 requires 32 rows of knitting to work one complete pattern repeat. In some of the more complex projects such as the fir trees tablecloth on page 40, specific sections of the pattern are repeated.

Where this is the case, the project instructions will tell you exactly which rows are to be repeated and which are to be worked once only.

When working a complicated stitch pattern, always make a note of exactly which row you are working. Use a row counter or write the row number in a notebook with a pencil as it's very easy to forget where you are when your knitting session gets interrupted by the doorbell or a telephone call. Avoid the temptation to use a pen when making notes as ink is rather messy and can be very difficult to remove from light-coloured yarn.

HOW TO FOLLOW A CHARTED PATTERN

Many knitters prefer working from a chart rather than from written instructions. Although a charted pattern still contains some written instructions, the most complicated part – the stitch pattern – is expressed in visual form. Traditionally, British patterns have been written rather than charted, but today there is a strong movement towards the charted stitch pattern which is used almost exclusively in other European countries. Charts also solve the problem of translating a long, complicated stitch pattern from one language to another.

To use a knitting chart, first familiarize yourself with the symbols and their meanings. These are given in the form of a key at the side of the chart. Each symbol represents a single instruction such as knit or purl, or a set of instructions such as knit two stitches together through the back of the loop. On some of the more complicated charts, such as the one for the pillowcase edging on page 34, some chart squares do not contain a symbol. These blank squares are used simply to make the chart a better shape and easier to follow.

Read knitting charts from the bottom, beginning at the right-hand edge of row 1 and working the first row from right to left across the chart. Work all the instructions on this row, then work row 2 from left to right in the same way. Read all the subsequent odd-numbered rows from right to left and even-numbered rows from left to

right. As a general rule, odd-numbered rows are right-side rows (the right side of the knitting is the one facing you as you work the row) and even-numbered rows are wrong-side rows (the back of the knitting is the one facing).

As when using written instructions, keep a note of which row you are working using a row counter or pad and pencil.

Knitting symbols
The chart shows the main symbols used in knitting charts. A key is also given beside each project and pattern library chart.

USING THE PATTERN LIBRARY

The pattern library pages give both written and charted instructions for a wide variety of stitch patterns. Many of these patterns can be substituted for project designs, particularly the edging and border patterns. A triangular raised leaf motif is given on page 76 which would make a lovely bedspread – work four motifs to make up each square and join the squares together in the same way as the Victorian bedspread on page 58. The large-scale lace patterns on page 68 can be substituted in the evening wrap on page 30.

To use the pattern library instructions, begin by casting on the correct number of stitches. For an edging, border or insertion, this number is given at the top of each pattern. Other patterns give you the correct number of stitches needed to work one complete pattern repeat. For example, the first line of the knotted trellis pattern on page 70 tells you to 'cast on a multiple of 6 sts plus 1'. This means that the total number of stitches to cast on so the pattern will be correct when knitted must be divisible by 6, and you must also add one extra stitch. So you could cast on say 61 stitches (6 × 10 + 1) or 73 (6 × 12 + 1) and the pattern would be correct in either case.

FINISHING TECHNIQUES

FINISHING OFF THREAD ENDS

Thread the end of the yarn through a tapestry needle and weave the point of the needle through several stitches on the wrong side of the knitting for at least 2.5 cm (1 in). Pull the needle and yarn through and cut off the yarn end.

PINNING OUT AND BLOCKING

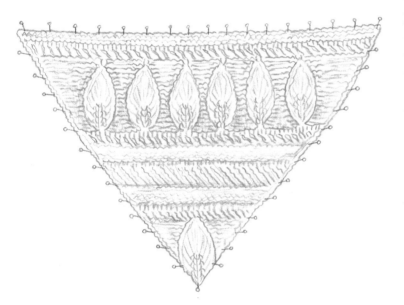

This process is essential for bringing out the delicate patterns in knitted lace and it can be used safely with either cotton, wool or wool/synthetic mixtures as no heat is applied. Although blocking may seem rather a lengthy process – a long strip may need pinning out in several sections and each section may take one or two days to dry out – the time will be well spent.

To pin out and block knitted lace you will need a large piece of blockboard or chipboard covered with thick cork floor tiles, brown paper, drawing pins, a sheet of polythene, stainless steel pins with glass or plastic heads and a small plant sprayer filled with cold water.

Using a pencil, draw the outline of the piece on to brown paper – for a border draw two parallel lines; for a circular piece, draw radiating lines from the centre corresponding with the number of motifs in the pattern; and for a square motif draw the correct size of square. Pin the brown paper on to the board with drawing pins and cover it with the polythene sheet.

Spray the knitting lightly with water and pin it out over the drawn shape using stainless steel pins. Adjust the pins until the knitting is stretched evenly, then spray with water once again, this time more heavily. Allow the knitting to dry completely at room temperature before removing the pins; the knitted fabric will retain the shape in which it dried. When blocking a border or edging, you will need to work in several sections, letting each portion of the work dry before moving on to the next section.

JOINING MOTIFS

After pinning and blocking all the knitted motifs to the same size, join them together by oversewing (see diagram) using the same yarn. Oversewing makes a very flat seam once it is opened out and pressed, unlike alternative methods which create an unsightly ridge.

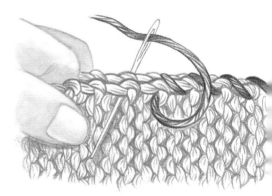

Place two motifs together with right sides facing and the two edges to be joined aligning. Oversew along the edge, securing the thread carefully at the beginning and end of the stitching. Repeat this with further motifs until you have a strip of joined motifs which is the required length. Open out the seams and press them lightly on the wrong side. Make as many strips as you require, then join them together with oversewing, taking care to match up the short seams neatly.

APPLYING BORDERS, EDGING AND INSERTIONS

A border to a knitted bedspread

Place the knitted border on top of the bedspread with right sides facing and straight edges aligning. Pin in place, distributing the length of the border evenly along the sides and gathering it slightly at each corner so that the border will lie flat without pulling. Use long pins with glass or plastic heads so the pinheads will not pull through the knitting. Using a tapestry needle and the same yarn that you used for the knitting, oversew the layers together.

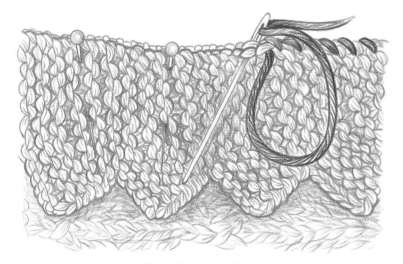

If you have used a very heavy yarn for the knitting, you will get a neater seam if you use a thinner thread, but don't be tempted to use sewing cotton as this will not be strong enough.

Attaching knitted lace edgings and borders to fabric

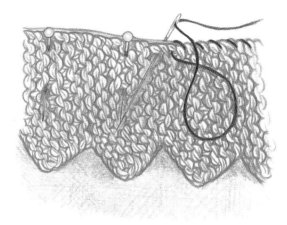

Position the edging or border on top of the hemmed edge of the fabric or towel with right sides facing and straight edges aligning. Make sure that the edging is evenly distributed and pin in place using glass-headed pins. Using a sewing needle and matching sewing cotton, stitch the knitting and fabric together using oversewing stitches. Make small, neat stitches and take care not to pull the thread too tightly as you work. When attaching the edging to a corner, gather the knitting slightly so that the edging will lie flat when stitched in position.

Adding knitted lace insertions

Insertions are sewn between two pieces of fabric and are often used in conjunction with an edging or border. Pin the top of the insertion to the first piece of fabric with right sides facing and proceed as above. Then pin the lower edge of the insertion to the second piece of fabric and apply in the same way.

CARING FOR AND STORING KNITTED LACE

Follow the cleaning and pressing instructions on the ball band for the particular yarn you are using – a list of the international care symbols found on ball bands is given on page 11. If the yarn you have used is machine-washable, put the item into a clean white pillowcase to prevent it from being damaged and stretched during the machine cycle.

When not in use, store knitted lace wrapped in white, acid-free tissue paper in a cool and dry place. When folding a large item, pad the folds with tissue paper to prevent hard creases forming or, better still, roll it right-side out round a cardboard tube between layers of tissue paper.

When a little care, you can use and enjoy the knitted lace items you have made for years to come. Follow these simple guidelines:
○ Always wash knitted lace before it gets really soiled, taking prompt action to remove stains as soon as they occur, particularly on table-linen.
○ Repair holes and split seams as soon as you notice them to prevent further damage to the piece.
○ Keep items out of direct sunlight, especially during summer, as the sunlight will not only cause colours to fade, but it will eventually weaken the fibres.

Starching knitted lace

Articles trimmed with knitted lace edgings benefit from being starched after laundering. Choose a stiff-finish starch for small items such as placemats and table runners and a soft-finish one for tablecloths, napkins and other items which will be draped or folded in use.

The best method is to use soluble starch mixed with water (follow the manufacturer's instructions). Dip the article into the solution, squeeze out the moisture, then allow it to dry. Finish by pressing the piece with a hot iron.

Spray starch works well with small knitted items, but take care when ironing as spray starch may scorch when using a very hot iron.

Projects in knitted lace

When selecting a project to make, choose one which reflects your present level of skill. Read right through the instructions before you begin to knit. You will also find it useful to work up one or more sample pieces to check the effect of your chosen yarn and hook. The following projects are aimed at people with varying levels of skill, from outright beginners to more experienced knitted lace enthusiasts. You'll find a symbol with one, two or three knitting needles at the start of each project. One needle indicates a very simple design, two indicates intermediate level and three needles are for more advanced projects which should only be attempted by a reader with considerable experience and patience.

EVENING WRAP

Soft, silky and glamorous, this evening wrap is knitted in a synthetic ribbon yarn, but you could substitute a pure wool yarn or a wool-and-mohair mixture, if you prefer. The eight-row pattern is not too difficult to knit and the work grows quickly on large needles. Four alternative patterns are given in the pattern library on page 71.

Never press ribbon yarn, even with a cool iron, as the synthetic fibres will quickly become flattened and limp. Instead, pin out the knitting in sections, spray with cold water and allow them to dry naturally.

Materials

Cream double-knitting weight ribbon yarn
Pair of 4.5 mm knitting needles
Large crochet hook
Stretching board and pins
Scissors

Measurements

The wrap shown here measures approximately 33 cm (13 in) wide and was worked across 72 stitches. It measures 150 cm (59 in) long, excluding the fringe.

To make the wrap wider or narrower, simply add or subtract 10 stitches for each pattern repeat.

Working the wrap

To make a neat selvedge at each side of the wrap, slip the first stitch of each row knitwise before working the instructions to the end of the row, then knit the stitch remaining on the needle through the back of the loop.

Abbreviations

A full list of knitting abbreviations is given on page 21.

Cast on a multiple of 10 sts plus 2 for selvedges.

ROW 1 * yo, k3, sl 1, k2 tog, psso, k3, yo, k1; rep from * to end.
ROW 2 AND EVERY ALT ROW Purl.
ROW 3 * K1, yo, k2, sl 1, k2 tog, psso, k2, yo, k2; rep from * to end.
ROW 5 * K2, yo, k1, sl 1, k2 tog, psso, k1, yo, k3; rep from * to end.
ROW 7 * K3, yo, sl 1, k2 tog, psso, yo, k4; rep from * to end.
ROW 8 Purl.
Repeat rows 1 to 8 until the wrap reaches the required length, ending with an 8th row.
Cast off loosely knitwise.

Finishing the wrap

1 Sew in the ends. Pin out the knitting following the illustrated instructions given on page 24. Spray lightly with water and allow to dry thoroughly before removing the pins. Do not press. You will probably need to pin out the wrap in several sections to accommodate it on your board.
2 Cut 60 cm (24 in) lengths of yarn. Using the crochet hook, thread groups of six lengths of yarn at regular 2.5 cm (1 in) intervals along the short edges of the wrap. Knot the ends to form a fringe. Trim the ends of the fringe to an even length.

This luxurious and glamorous evening wrap can be worked in various yarns or wools. Here, it is knitted in ribbon yarn. Make a more elaborate fringe by knotting beads on to the strands.

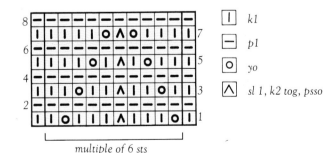

multiple of 6 sts

⎸	k1
—	p1
○	yo
⋀	sl 1, k2 tog, psso

SCENTED SACHETS

Scented sachets make a delightful birthday or Christmas gift. These two sachets are made from white cotton fabric with a delicate woven pattern, but you could use scraps of printed cotton lawn and pick up the dominant print colour with the ribbon threaded through the edging. Here, a synthetic ribbon yarn is used to knit the edging, but almost any type of cotton or synthetic yarn could be substituted.
Fill the sachets with a little stuffing and a strongly scented pot pourri, such as dried rose petals.

Materials
Cream double knitting weight ribbon
    yarn
Scraps of self-patterned white cotton
    fabric
Pair of 3.5 mm knitting needles
Narrow white satin ribbon
Matching sewing thread
Sewing needle
Pins
Small amount of white polyester stuff-
    ing
Pot pourri

Measurements
Cut out two circles of fabric approxi-mately 10 cm (4 in) in diameter for the sachet with the wide edging and two of the same size for the other sachet. The fin-ished size of the sachet centres will be 8 cm (3 in) across and there is a seam allowance of 1 cm (½ in) all round. Knit the edging long enough to go round the circumfer-ence of the finished piece.

Abbreviations
A full list of knitting abbreviations is given on page 21.
Special abbreviation for this pattern:
inc = knit once onto the front and once into the back of the next stitch.

Working the wide edging
Cast on 8 sts and knit 1 row.
ROW 1 Sl 1, k2, [yo, k2 tog] twice, inc in last st.
ROWS 2, 4 AND 6 Knit.
ROW 3 Sl 1, k2, yo, k2 tog, k1, yo, k2 tog, inc in last st.
ROW 5 Sl 1, k2, yo, k2 tog, k2, yo, k2 tog, inc in last st.
ROW 7 Sl 1, k2, yo, k2 tog, k3, yo, k2 tog, inc in last st.
ROW 8 Cast off 4 sts, k7.
Repeat rows 1 to 8 until the edging is the required length, ending with an 8th row.
Cast off loosely knitwise.

Working the narrow edging
Cast on 5 sts and knit 1 row
ROW 1 Sl 1, k1, yo, k2 tog, inc in last st.
ROWS 2, 4 AND 6 Knit.
ROW 3 Sl 1, k2, yo, k2 tog, inc in last st.
ROW 5 Sl 1, k3, yo, k2 tog, inc in last st.
ROW 7 Sl 1, k4, yo, k2 tog, inc in last st.
ROW 8 Cast off 4 sts, k4.
Repeat rows 1 to 8 until the edging is the required length, ending with an 8th row.
Cast off loosely knitwise.

Making up the sachets
Both designs are made as follows:
1 Sew in the ends. Pin out the edging following the illustrated instructions given on page 24. Spray lightly with water and allow to dry completely before removing the pins. Do not press the ribbon yarn.
2 Pin two fabric circles together with right sides facing and machine stitch round the

Rich cream ribbon yarn edges these little sachets filled with scented pot pourri. They are very easy to knit and make an excellent beginner's project.

edge with a 1 cm (½ in) seam allowance, leaving a short opening for turning. Cut small notches into the raw edges, taking care not to cut into the stitching. Turn out through the opening and press lightly.

3 Fill the sachet with a mixture of polyester stuffing and pot pourri, then slipstitch the opening closed.

4 Pin the knitted edging evenly along the seam round the sachet and stitch in place using matching thread. Join the edges of the knitting in the same way. Thread the ribbon through a row of holes in the edging and tie into a neat bow.

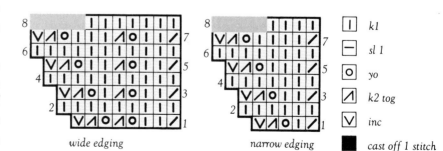

wide edging   *narrow edging*

	k1
−	sl 1
o	yo
⋀	k2 tog
V	inc
■	cast off 1 stitch

WEDDING GIFT
BED LINEN

This unusual knitted edging decorates a pair of pristine white linen pillowcases to make a luxurious wedding gift for a special friend or relative. The edging is worked in fine cotton yarn and you can also make a longer matching strip to edge the top of a flat sheet. Instructions and charts for four simpler knitted edgings are given on page 64 of the pattern library, and any of those could be substituted for the intricate design shown here. For knitters who find working with this weight of yarn a daunting and time-consuming task, why not knit two short strips of the edging pattern using double knitting weight cotton yarn and use them to trim a pair of white hand towels? When working your edging, choose a slightly larger needle size than usual as this pattern works best when the tension is fairly loose. You may need to knit several samples before finding the right combination.

Materials
White fine cotton yarn
Pair of white cotton or linen pillowcases
Pair of 3.25 mm knitting needles
Matching sewing thread
Sewing needle
Pins

Measurements
The original knitted edging measures approximately 6.5 cm (2½ in) across the widest point. For each pillowcase you will need to knit one strip of edging which is long enough to stretch right round the edge of the pillowcase and be gathered at each corner. To edge a flat sheet, work pattern repeats until your edging reaches the desired length.

Abbreviations
A full list of knitting abbreviations is given on page 21.
Special abbreviations for this pattern:
loop = cast on one stitch, then knit this stitch and the next stitch on the left-hand needle together wrapping the yarn twice round the needle
tog2 = knit the next two stitches on the left-hand needle together wrapping the yarn twice round the needle, then knit into the front of the first stitch again
inc1 = knit into the front and the back of the next stitch
yf = yarn forward to make a stitch
yrn2 = yarn round the needle twice
po = on left-hand needle, pass fourth, fifth and sixth stitches (in that order) over the first, second and third stitches and off the needle. When working yrn2 (yarn round the needle twice) it must be noted that on the following row this must have a k1 and p1 worked into the corresponding loops.

Working the edging
Cast on 26 sts.
ROW 1 (Right side facing) loop, k18, inc1, k6.
ROW 2 K4, p6, k17 dropping extra loop made on previous row.
ROW 3 Loop, k26.
ROW 4 Rep row 2.
ROW 5 Loop, k13, yf, k3, po, yrn2, k7.
ROW 6 K4, p3, k1, p1, k18 dropping extra loop made on previous row.
ROW 7 Loop, k19, inc1, k6.
ROW 8 K4, p6, k18 dropping extra loop made on previous row.

A treasured gift for the bridal couple, this exquisite bed linen is edged in a fine cotton yarn knitted at a fairly loose tension.

ROW 9 Loop, k12, yf, tog2, yf, k13.

ROW 10 K4, p6, k20 dropping extra loops made on previous row.

ROW 11 Loop, k12, turn.

ROW 12 K13 dropping extra loop made on previous row.

ROW 13 Loop, k11, k next 2 sts together but knitting into the front of both sts and then into the front of the first st again, k6, po, yrn 2, k7.

ROW 14 K4, p3, k1, p1, k20 dropping extra loop made on previous row.

ROW 15 Loop, k12, yf, [tog2, yf] twice, k5, inc1, k6.

ROW 16 K4, p6, k23 dropping extra loops made on previous row.

ROW 17 Loop, k32.

ROW 18 K4, p6, k23 dropping extra loop made on previous row.

ROW 19 Rep row 11.

ROW 20 Rep row 12.

ROW 21 Loop, k11, k next 2 sts together but knitting into the front of both sts and then into the front of the first st again, yf, [tog2, yf] 3 times, k3, po, yrn2, k7.

ROW 22 K4, p3, k1, p1, k16 dropping extra loops made on previous row, now working on sts on left-hand needle, pass 2nd, 3rd, 4th, 5th, 6th, 7th, 8th, 9th and 10th sts over first st, now k tog this first st with last st on needle dropping extra loop made on previous row. (26 sts)

Repeat these 22 rows for length of edging required, ending with a 22nd row.

Cast off loosely.

Attaching the edging

1 Pin out the edging in sections following the illustrated instructions given on page 24. Spray with water and allow to dry completely before removing the pins and moving on to the next section.

2 Pin the edging around the edge of the pillowcase, gently gathering the corners to fit and making sure you space out the edging evenly. Oversew the edging in place with matching sewing thread, taking care not to pull the stitches tight, then oversew the cast-on and cast-off edges together.

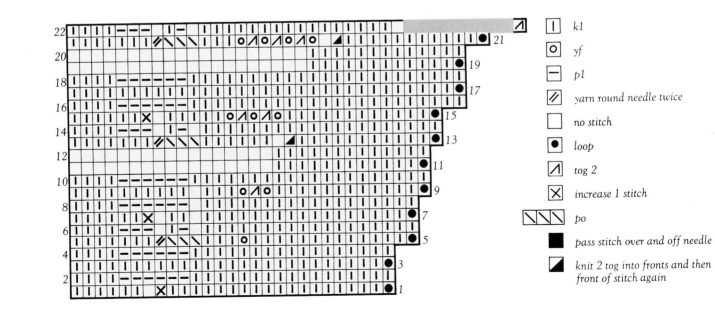

Symbol	Meaning
I	k1
o	yf
−	p1
⁄⁄	yarn round needle twice
□	no stitch
●	loop
⊿	tog 2
X	increase 1 stitch
\\\\\\	po
■	pass stitch over and off needle
◢	knit 2 tog into fronts and then front of stitch again

LACE-EDGED HANDKERCHIEF

Ready-made handkerchiefs are easily decorated with a narrow edging knitted in fine cotton yarn. Here, a beautifully embroidered handkerchief has been trimmed with a simple-to-knit, delicate edging. However, this edging would look equally effective on a plain white cotton or linen square.

When knitting the edging, remember to allow a little extra length so that it can be gathered at each corner; this will allow it to lie flat when stitched in place. The same edging can be used to decorate lingerie, nightwear and children's clothes.

Materials
White fine cotton yarn
White cotton or linen handkerchief
Pair of 2.5 mm knitting needles
Matching sewing thread
Sewing needle
Pins

Measurements
You will need to knit a strip of edging to go round the outside edge of the handker-chief, allowing a little extra so that the edging can be gathered slightly at each corner when it is stitched in place.

Abbreviations
Knitting abbreviations appear on page 21.

A delicate edging borders a beautiful cotton handkerchief. The pattern is easy to knit and can be used to edge a number of other small items.

Working the edging

Cast on 6 sts.

ROW 1 Sl 1, k1, yo, k2 tog, yo twice, k2.

ROW 2 Sl 1, k2, p1, k4.

ROW 3 Sl 1, k1, yo, k2 tog, k4.

ROW 4 [Sl 1, k1, psso] twice, k4.

Repeat rows 1 to 4 until the edging is the required length, ending with a 4th row.

Cast off loosely knitwise.

Attaching the edging

1 Sew in the ends. Pin out the edging following the illustrated instructions given on page 24. Spray lightly with water and allow to dry completely before removing the pins.

2 Beginning at the centre of one side, pin the edging right round the edge of the handkerchief, allowing a little extra at each corner so the edging can be slightly gathered round the point.

3 Oversew the edging in place with matching sewing thread, taking care not to pull the stitches tight. Join the short ends of the knitting in the same way.

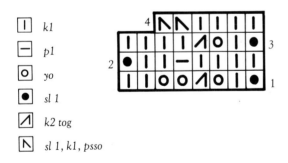

	k1
	p1
	yo
	sl 1
	k2 tog
	sl 1, k1, psso

CRYSTAL JAR COVER

A hand-cut crystal jar with silver-edged glass lid provides the perfect place for displaying a tiny piece of delicate lace knitting. The pattern shown here is perfectly suitable for a beginner to work, especially as no shaping is involved.

Starch your finished piece of knitting stiffly before pinning it out and allow it to dry thoroughly before trimming and mounting it in the lid surround. Here we have used cream yarn backed with a pastel paper, but you may prefer to choose a brightly coloured yarn and show off the knitting against a darker background.

Materials

Cream fine cotton yarn

Crystal jar with self-assembly lid (see page 78)

Pair of 2.5 mm knitting needles

Stiff-finish starch

Scrap of coloured paper about 2.5 cm (1 in) larger than the jar lid

Scissors to cut knitting and paper

Measurements

You will need to knit a piece of lace approximately 2.5 cm (1 in) larger all round than your jar lid. Use the acetate from the lid as a template around which to cut the finished piece of knitting. Don't worry if the piece turns out much larger than the lid as any surplus can be cut away quite easily after you have starched and pinned out the lace.

Abbreviations
Knitting abbreviations appear on page 21.

Working the lace
Cast on a multiple of 6 sts plus 1. K1 row.
ROW 1 AND EVERY ALT ROW Purl.
ROWS 2, 4 AND 6 K1, * yo, sl 1, k1, psso, k1, k2 tog, yo, k1; rep from * to end.
ROW 8 K2, * yo, sl 1, k2 tog, psso, yo, k3; rep from *, ending last rep k2.
ROW 10 K1, * k2 tog, yo, k1, yo, sl 1, k1, psso, k1; rep from * to end.
ROW 12 K2 tog, * yo, k3, yo, sl 1, k2 tog, psso; rep from *, ending last rep yo, k3, yo, sl 1, k1, psso.
Repeat rows 1 to 12 until knitting is required length, ending with a 12th row. Cast off loosely knitwise.

Mounting the lace
1 Starch the lace stiffly. Pin out following the illustrated instructions on page 24 and allow to dry completely before removing the pins.

2 Centre the acetate from the jar lid on top of the stiffened lace and cut out the lace carefully, close to the edge. Cut out a piece of coloured paper in the same way.
3 Position the acetate inside the lid surround and cover it with the lace circle, placing it so the right side of the knitting is next to the acetate. Finally, add the coloured paper and backing piece. Carefully secure all the layers in the lid.

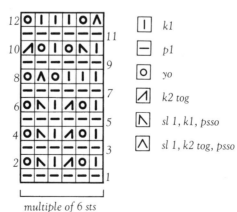

multiple of 6 sts

	k1
	p1
	yo
	k2 tog
	sl 1, k1, psso
	sl 1, k2 tog, psso

FIR TREES TABLECLOTH

Make this pretty knitted border with its pattern of fir trees to edge a plain or lightly embroidered square tablecloth. The border appears deceptively simple but owing to its complex shaping and intricate edging it should only be attempted by the experienced knitter. As the border has shaped corners, you must knit the edging to the required size first, then cut your fabric to fit.

Materials
White fine mercerized cotton, No 40 or
    finer
White cotton or linen fabric
Pair of 2 mm knitting needles
White sewing thread
Sewing needle
Pins

Measurements
The border is made up of four identical pieces (see diagram). The original border measures 11 cm (4¼ in) at the widest point and each side contains 21 repeats of the centre 36-row portion of the chart.

Abbreviations
Knitting abbreviations appear on page 21.
Special abbreviations for this pattern:
yf = yarn forward
inc = knit into the front and then the back of the next stitch
yrn3 = yarn round needle three times. When working yrn3, the following row must have a k1, p1, k1 worked into the corresponding loops.

Working the border (make 4)
Cast on 4 sts.
ROW 1 *(RIGHT SIDE FACING)* Inc in first st, yrn3, k2 tog, inc in last st.
ROW 2 Inc in first st, k3, p1, k2, inc in last st.
ROW 3 Inc in first st, k6, k2 tog, k1.
ROW 4 K2 tog, using st on right-hand needle cast off 2 sts, k2, k2 tog, yf, k1, inc in last st.
ROW 5 Inc in first st, k4, yrn 3, k2 tog, inc in last st.
ROW 6 Inc in first st, k3, p1, k1, [k2 tog, yf] twice, k1, inc in last st.
ROW 7 Inc in first st, k10, k2 tog, k1.
ROW 8 K2 tog, using st on right-hand needle cast off 2 sts, k2, [k2 tog, yf] 3 times, k1, inc in last st.
ROW 9 Inc in first st, k8, yrn3, k2 tog, inc in last st.
ROW 10 Inc in first st, k3, p1, k1, [k2 tog, yf] 4 times, k1, inc in last st.
ROW 11 Inc in first st, k14, k2 tog, k1.
ROW 12 K2 tog, using st on right-hand needle cast off 2 sts, k2, [k2 tog, yf] 5 times, k2.
ROW 13 Inc in first st, k11, yrn3, k2 tog, inc in last st.
ROW 14 Inc in first st, k3, p1, k1, [k2 tog, yf] 6 times, k1.
ROW 15 Inc in first st, k16, k2 tog, k1.
ROW 16 K2 tog, using st on right-hand needle cast off 2 sts, k2, [k2 tog, yf] 6 times, k2.
ROW 17 Inc in first st, k13, yrn3, k2 tog, inc in last st.
ROW 18 Inc in first st, k3, p1, k1, [k2 tog, yf] 6 times, k3.
ROW 19 Inc in first st, k18, k2 tog, k1.
ROW 20 K2 tog, using st on right-hand needle cast off 2 sts, k2, [k2 tog, yf] 5 times, k6.
ROW 21 Inc in first st, k15, yrn3, k2 tog, inc in last st.
ROW 22 Inc in first st, k3, p1, k1, [k2 tog, yf] 4 times, k9.

This deep fir trees border is a challenge for the seasoned knitter, but the finished result is well worth the effort. The pattern is knitted in fine cotton.

ROW 23 Inc in first st, k20, k2 tog, k1.

ROW 24 K2 tog, using st on right-hand needle cast off 2 sts, k2, [k2 tog, yf] 3 times, k12.

ROW 25 Inc in first st, k17, yrn3, k2 tog, inc in last st.

ROW 26 Inc in first st, k3, p1, k1, [k2 tog, yf] twice, k15.

ROW 27 Inc in first st, k22, k2 tog, k1.

ROW 28 K2 tog, using st on right-hand needle cast off 2 sts, k2, k2 tog, yf, k18.

ROW 29 Inc in first st, k19, yrn3, k2 tog, inc in last st.

ROW 30 Inc in first st, k3, p1, k9, [k2 tog, yf] 6 times, k1.

ROW 31 Inc in first st, k24, k2 tog, k1.

ROW 32 K2 tog, using st on right-hand needle cast off 2 sts, k3, yf, k21.

ROW 33 Inc in first st, k18, k2 tog, k2, yrn3, k2 tog, inc in last st.

ROW 34 Inc in first st, k3, p1, k2, yf, k2 tog, yf, k20.

ROW 35 Inc in first st, k17, k2 tog, k8, k2 tog, k1.

ROW 36 K2 tog, using st on right-hand needle cast off 2 sts, k3, [yf, k2 tog] twice, yf, k19.

ROW 37 Inc in first st, yf, k2 tog, k14, k2 tog, k6, yrn3, k2 tog, inc in last st.

ROW 38 Inc in first st, k3, p1, k2, [yf, k2 tog] 3 times, yf, k18.

ROW 39 Inc in first st, k1, yf, [k2 tog, k12] twice, k2 tog, k1.

ROW 40 K2 tog, using st on right-hand needle cast off 2 sts, k3, [yf, k2 tog] 4 times, yf, k14, yf, k2 tog, k1.

ROW 41 Inc in first st, k2, yf, [k2 tog, k10] twice, yrn3, k2 tog, inc in last st.

ROW 42 Inc in first st, k3, p1, k2, [yf, k2 tog] 5 times, yf, k12, yf, k2 tog, k2.

ROW 43 Inc in first st, k3, yf, k2 tog, k8, k2 tog, k16, k2 tog, k1.

ROW 44 K2 tog, using st on right-hand needle cast off 2 sts, k3, [yf, k2 tog] 6 times, yf, k10, yf, k2 tog, k3.

ROW 45 Inc in first st, k4, yf, k2 tog, k6, k2 tog, k14, yrn3, k2 tog, inc in last st.

ROW 46 Inc in first st, k3, p1, k2, [yf, k2 tog] 7 times, yf, k8, yf, k2 tog, k4.

ROW 47 Inc in first st, k5, yf, k2 tog, k4, k2 tog, k20, k2 tog, k1.

ROW 48 K2 tog, using st on right-hand needle cast off 2 sts, k3, [yf, k2 tog] 8 times, yf, k6, yf, [k2 tog] twice, k3.

ROW 49 Inc in first st, k1, yrn3, k2 tog, k2, yf, [k2 tog] twice, k18, yrn3, k2 tog, inc in last st.

ROW 50 Inc in first st, k3, p1, k1, [k2 tog, yf] 8 times, k7, yf, k2 tog, k2, p1, k4.

ROW 51 Inc in first st, k8, yf, k2 tog, k25, k2 tog, k1.

ROW 52 K2 tog, using st on right-hand needle cast off 2 sts, k2, [k2 tog, yf] 7 times, k9, yf, [k2 tog] twice, k6.

ROW 53 Inc in first st, yf, [k2 tog] twice, yrn3, k2 tog, k2, yf, k2 tog, k21, yrn3, k2 tog, inc in last st.

ROW 54 Inc in first st, k3, p1, k1, [k2 tog, yf] 6 times, k11, yf, k2 tog, k2, p1, k4, yf, k2 tog.

ROW 55 Inc in first st, k1, yf, k2 tog, k7, yf, k2 tog, k25, k2 tog, k1.

ROW 56 K2 tog, using st on right-hand needle cast off 2 sts, k2, [k2 tog, yf] 5 times, k13, yf, [k2 tog] twice, k5, yf, k2 tog, k1.

The shaping of the first corner is now complete. Now begin the centre section:

ROW 57 Sl 1, k2, yf, [k2 tog] twice, yrn3, k2 tog, k2, yf, k2 tog, k21, yrn3, k2 tog, inc in last st.

ROW 58 Inc in first st, k3, p1, k1, [k2 tog, yf] 4 times, k15, yf, k2 tog, k2, p1, k4, yf, k2 tog, k1.

ROW 59 Sl 1, k2, yf, k2 tog, k7, yf, k2 tog, k25, k2 tog, k1.

ROW 60 K2 tog, using st on right-hand needle cast off 2 sts, k2, [k2 tog, yf] 3 times, k17, yf, [k2 tog] twice, k5, yf, k2 tog, k1.

ROW 61 Sl 1, k2, yf, [k2 tog] twice, yrn3,

k2 tog, k2, yf, k2 tog, k21, yrn3, k2 tog, inc in last st.

ROW 62 Inc in first st, k3, p1, k1, [k2 tog, yf] twice, k19, yf, k2 tog, k2, p1, k4, yf, k2 tog, k1.

ROW 63 Sl 1, k2, yf, k2 tog, k7, yf, k2 tog, k25, k2 tog, k1.

ROW 64 K2 tog, using st on right-hand needle cast off 2 sts, k2, k2 tog, yf, k21, yf, [k2 tog] twice, k5, yf, k2 tog, k1.

Now work the following 36 rows which form the pattern repeat:

ROW 1 (RIGHT SIDE FACING) Sl 1, k2, yf, [k2 tog] twice, yrn3, k2 tog, k2, yf, k2 tog, k21, yrn3, k2 tog, inc in last st.

ROW 2 Inc in first st, k3, p1, k9, [k2 tog, yf] 6 times, k3, yf, k2 tog, k2, p1, k4, yf, k2 tog, k1.

ROW 3 Sl 1, k2, yf, k2 tog, k7, yf, k2 tog, k25, k2 tog, k1.

ROW 4 K2 tog, using st on right-hand needle cast off 2 sts, k3, yf, k22, yf, [k2 tog] twice, k5, yf, k2 tog, k1.

ROW 5 Sl 1, k2, yf, [k2 tog] twice, yrn3, k2 tog, k2, yf, k2 tog, k18, k2 tog, k2, yrn3, k2 tog, inc in last st.

ROW 6 Inc in first st, k3, p1, k2, yf, k2 tog, yf, k20, yf, k2 tog, k2, p1, k4, yf, k2 tog, k1.

ROW 7 Sl 1, k2, yf, k2 tog, k7, yf, k2 tog, k16, k2 tog, k8, k2 tog, k1.

ROW 8 K2 tog, using st on right-hand needle cast off 2 sts, k3, yf, [k2 tog, yf] twice, k18, yf, [k2 tog] twice, k5, yf, k2 tog, k1.

ROW 9 Sl 1, k2, yf, [k2 tog] twice, yrn3, k2 tog, k2, yf, k2 tog, k14, k2 tog, k6, yrn3, k2 tog, inc in last st.

ROW 10 Inc in first st, k3, p1, k2, yf, [k2 tog, yf] 3 times, k16, yf, k2 tog, k2, p1, k4, yf, k2 tog, k1.

ROW 11 Sl 1, k2, yf, k2 tog, k7, yf, [k2 tog, k12] twice, k2 tog, k1.

ROW 12 K2 tog, using st on right-hand needle cast off 2 sts, k3, yf, [k2 tog, yf] 4 times, k14, yf, [k2 tog] twice, k5, yf, k2 tog, k1.

ROW 13 Sl 1, k2, yf, [k2 tog] twice, yrn3, k2 tog, k2, yf, [k2 tog, k10] twice, yrn3, k2 tog, inc in last st.

ROW 14 Inc in first st, k3, p1, k2, yf, [k2 tog, yf] 5 times, k12, yf, k2 tog, k2, p1, k4, yf, k2 tog, k1.

ROW 15 Sl 1, k2, yf, k2 tog, k7, yf, k2 tog, k8, k2 tog, k16, k2 tog, k1.

ROW 16 K2 tog, using st on right-hand needle cast off 2 sts, k3, yf, [k2 tog, yf] 6 times, k10, yf, [k2 tog] twice, k5, yf, k2 tog, k1.

ROW 17 Sl 1, k2, yf, [k2 tog] twice, yrn3, k2 tog, k2, yf, k2 tog, k6, k2 tog, k14, yrn3, k2 tog, inc in last st.

ROW 18 Inc in first st, k3, p1, k2, yf, [k2 tog, yf] 7 times, k8, yf, k2 tog, k2, p1, k4, yf, k2 tog, k1.

ROW 19 Sl 1, k2, yf, k2 tog, k7, yf, k2 tog, k4, k2 tog, k20, k2 tog, k1.

ROW 20 K2 tog, using st on right-hand needle cast off 2 sts, k3, yf, [k2 tog, yf] 8 times, k6, yf, [k2 tog] twice, k5, yf, k2 tog, k1.

ROW 21 Sl 1, k2, yf, [k2 tog] twice, yrn3, k2 tog, k2, yf, k2 tog, k2, k2 tog, k18, yrn3, k2 tog, inc in last st.

ROW 22 Inc in first st, k3, p1, k1, [k2 tog, yf] 8 times, k7, yf, k2 tog, k2, p1, k4, yf, k2 tog, k1.

ROW 23 Sl 1, k2, yf, k2 tog, k7, yf, k2 tog, k25, k2 tog, k1.

ROW 24 K2 tog, using st on right-hand needle cast off 2 sts, k2, [k2 tog, yf] 7 times, k9, yf, [k2 tog] twice, k5, yf, k2 tog, k1.

ROW 25 Sl 1, k2, yf, [k2 tog] twice, yrn3, k2 tog, k2, yf, k2 tog, k21, yrn3, k2 tog, inc in last st.

ROW 26 Inc in first st, k3, p1, k1, [k2 tog, yf] 6 times, k11, yf, k2 tog, k2, p1, k4, yf, k2 tog, k1.

ROW 27 Sl 1, k2, yf, k2 tog, k7, yf, k2 tog, k25, k2 tog, k1.

ROW 28 K2 tog, using st on right-hand needle cast off 2 sts, k2, [k2 tog, yf] 5 times, k13, yf, [k2 tog] twice, k5, yf, k2 tog, k1.

ROW 29 Sl 1, k2, yf, [k2 tog] twice, yrn3, k2 tog, k2, yf, k2 tog, k21, yrn3, k2 tog, inc in last st.

ROW 30 Inc in first st, k3, p1, k1, [k2 tog, yf] 4 times, k15, yf, k2 tog, k2, p1, k4, yf, k2 tog, k1.

ROW 31 Sl 1, k2, yf, k2 tog, k7, yf, k2 tog, k25, k2 tog, k1.

ROW 32 K2 tog, using st on right-hand needle cast off 2 sts, k2, [k2 tog, yf] 3 times, k17, yf, [k2 tog] twice, k5, yf, k2 tog, k1.

ROW 33 Sl 1, k2, yf, [k2 tog] twice, yrn3, k2 tog, k2, yf, k2 tog, k21, yrn3, k2 tog, inc in last st.

ROW 34 Inc in first st, k3, p1, k1, [k2 tog, yf] twice, k19, yf, k2 tog, k2, p1, k4, yf, k2 tog, k1.

ROW 35 Sl 1, k2, yf, k2 tog, k7, yf, k2 tog, k25, k2 tog, k1.

ROW 36 K2 tog, using st on right-hand needle cast off 2 sts, k2, k2 tog, yf, k21, yf, [k2 tog] twice, k5, yf, k2 tog, k1.
Repeat last 36 rows 21 times, or as many times as necessary. Then work rows 1 to 10 again.

Now start the decrease of the border:
ROW 1 (RS FACING) K2 tog, k1, yf, k2 tog, k7, yf, [k2 tog, k12] twice, k2 tog, k1.

ROW 2 K2 tog, using st on right-hand needle cast off 2 sts, k3, yf, [k2 tog, yf] 4 times, k14, yf, [k2 tog] twice, k5, yf, k2 tog.

ROW 3 K2 tog, yf, [k2 tog] twice, yrn3, k2 tog, k2, yf, [k2 tog, k10] twice, yrn3, k2 tog, inc in last st.

ROW 4 Inc in first st, k3, p1, k2, yf, [k2 tog, yf] 5 times, k12, yf, k2 tog, k2, p1, k5.

	k1
o	yf
⋀	k2 tog
−	p1
●	slip 1 stitch
X	increase 1 stitch
▨	yarn round needle 3 times
	no stitch
■	cast off stitch

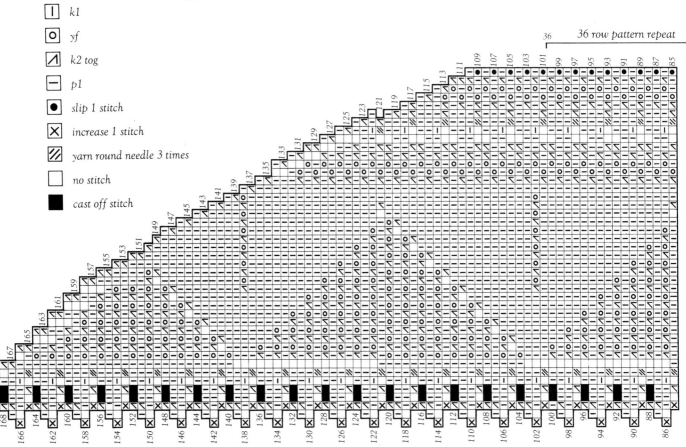

36 row pattern repeat

ROW 5 K2 tog, k8, yf, k2 tog, k8, k2 tog, k16, k2 tog, k1.

ROW 6 K2 tog, using st on right-hand needle cast off 2 sts, k3, yf, [k2 tog, yf] 6 times, k10, yf, [k2 tog] twice, k5.

ROW 7 [K2 tog] twice, yrn3, k2 tog, k2, yf, k2 tog, k6, k2 tog, k14, yrn3, k2 tog, inc in last st.

ROW 8 Inc in first st, k3, p1, k2, yf, [k2 tog, yf] 7 times, k8, yf, k2 tog, k2, p1, k3.

ROW 9 K2 tog, k6, yf, k2 tog, k4, k2 tog, k20, k2 tog, k1.

ROW 10 K2 tog, using st on right-hand needle cast off 2 sts, k3, yf, [k2 tog, yf] 8 times, k6, yf, [k2 tog] twice, k3.

ROW 11 K2 tog, yrn3, k2 tog, k2, yf, k2 tog, k2, k2 tog, k18, yrn3, k2 tog, inc in last st.

ROW 12 Inc in first st, k3, p1, k1, [k2 tog, yf] 8 times, k7, yf, k2 tog, k2, p1, k2.

ROW 13 K2 tog, k5, yf, k2 tog, k25, k2 tog, k1.

ROW 14 K2 tog, using st on right-hand needle cast off 2 sts, k2, [k2 tog, yf] 7 times, k9, yf, [k2 tog] twice, k2.

ROW 15 K2 tog, k3, yf, k2 tog, k21, yrn3, k2 tog, inc in last st.

ROW 16 Inc in first st, k3, p1, k1, [k2 tog, yf] 6 times, k11, yf, k2 tog, k2.

ROW 17 K2 tog, k2, yf, k2 tog, k25, k2 tog, k1.

ROW 18 K2 tog, using st on right-hand needle cast off 2 sts, k2, [k2 tog, yf] 5 times, k13, yf, k2 tog, k1.

ROW 19 K2 tog, k1, yf, k2 tog, k21, yrn3, k2 tog, inc in last st.

ROW 20 Inc in first st, k3, p1, k1, [k2 tog, yf] 4 times, k15, yf, k2 tog.

ROW 21 K2 tog, yf, k2 tog, k25, k2 tog, k1.

ROW 22 K2 tog, using st on right-hand needle cast off 2 sts, k2, [k2 tog, yf] 3 times, k18.

ROW 23 K2 tog, k22, yrn3, k2 tog, inc in last st.

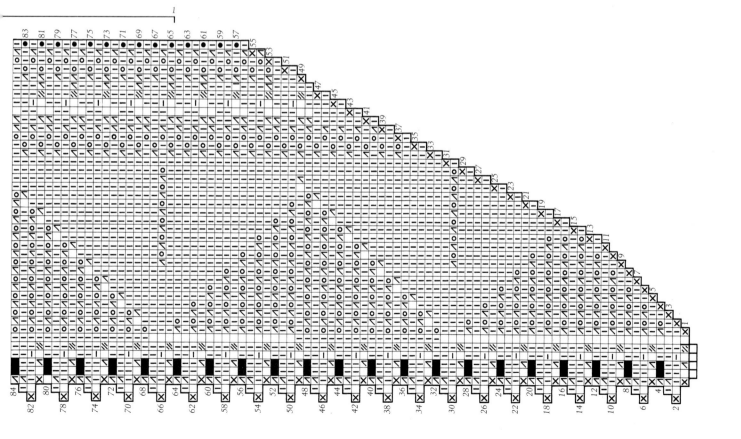

ROW 24 Inc in first st, k3, p1, k1, [k2 tog, yf] twice, k19.

ROW 25 K2 tog, k25, k2 tog, k1.

ROW 26 K2 tog, using st on right-hand needle cast off 2 sts, k2, k2 tog, yf, k20.

ROW 27 K2 tog, k20, yrn3, k2 tog, inc in last st.

ROW 28 Inc in first st, k3, p1, k9, [k2 tog, yf] 6 times, k1.

ROW 29 K2 tog, k23, k2 tog, k1.

ROW 30 K2 tog, using st on right-hand needle cast off 2 sts, k3, yf, k19.

ROW 31 K2 tog, k15, k2 tog, k2, yrn3, k2 tog, inc in last st.

ROW 32 Inc in first st, k3, p1, k2, yf, k2 tog, yf, k16.

ROW 33 K2 tog, k12, k2 tog, k8, k2 tog, k1.

ROW 34 K2 tog, using st on right-hand needle cast off 2 sts, k3, yf, [k2 tog, yf] twice, k13.

ROW 35 K2 tog, k9, k2 tog, k6, yrn3, k2 tog, inc in last st.

ROW 36 Inc in first st, k3, p1, k2, yf, [k2 tog, yf] 3 times, k10.

ROW 37 K2 tog, k6, k2 tog, k12, k2 tog, k1.

ROW 38 K2 tog, using st on right-hand needle cast off 2 sts, k3, yf, [k2 tog, yf] 4 times, k7.

ROW 39 K2 tog, k3, k2 tog, k10, yrn3, k2 tog, inc in last st.

ROW 40 Inc in first st, k3, p1, k2, yf, [k2 tog, yf] 5 times, k2, k2 tog.

ROW 41 K2 tog, k17, k2 tog, k1.

ROW 42 K2 tog, using st on right-hand needle cast off 2 sts, k3, yf, [k2 tog, yf] 4 times, k3, k2 tog.

ROW 43 K2 tog, k12, yrn3, k2 tog, inc in last st.

ROW 44 Inc in first st, k3, p1, k2, yf, [k2 tog, yf] 4 times, k2, k2 tog.

ROW 45 K2 tog, k15, k2 tog, k1.

ROW 46 K2 tog, using st on right-hand needle cast off 2 sts, k3, yf, [k2 tog, yf] 3 times, k2 tog, k1, k2 tog.

ROW 47 K2 tog, k9, yrn3, k2 tog, inc in last st.

ROW 48 Inc in first st, k3, p1, k2, yf, [k2 tog, yf] twice, k2 tog, k1, k2 tog.

ROW 49 K2 tog, k11, k2 tog, k1.

ROW 50 K2 tog, using st on right-hand needle cast off 2 sts, k3, [yf, k2 tog] twice, k1, k2 tog.

ROW 51 K2 tog, k5, yrn3, k2 tog, inc in last st.

ROW 52 Inc in first st, k3, p1, k2, yf, k2 tog, k1, k2 tog.

ROW 53 K2 tog, k7, k2 tog, k1.

ROW 54 K2 tog, using st on right-hand needle cast off 2 sts, k3, yf, k1, k2 tog.

ROW 55 K2 tog, k2, yrn3, k2 tog, inc in last st.

ROW 56 Inc in first st, k3, p1, k2, k2 tog.

ROW 57 K2 tog, k4, k2 tog, k1.

ROW 58 K2 tog, using st on right-hand needle cast off 2 sts, k1, k2 tog (3 sts). Cast off rem 3 sts.

Making up the tablecloth

1 Sew in the ends. Pin out the border a section at a time following the instructions given on page 24, taking special care with the corner sections. Spray with water and allow each section to dry before moving on to the next section.

2 Join the short ends of the border, matching the pattern carefully and using small, neat stitches and matching sewing thread. Pin the border roughly on to the fabric, making sure that the fir tree motifs are evenly spaced along each side. Carefully trim the fabric to fit, allowing a 3 cm (1¼ in) hem allowance all round. Remove the pins. Turn, pin and tack a double 1.5 cm (⅝ in) hem round the cloth. Hand or machine-stitch using matching thread.

3 Pin the border round the cloth, spacing the motifs evenly. Using small, neat stitches and matching sewing thread, oversew the border to the tablecloth. Finally, press lightly on the wrong side with a warm iron.

CIRCULAR TEA CLOTH

This delightful circular cloth features a lace petal and leaf design set off with a feather-and-fan border. It is knitted in rounds from the centre outwards. Begin by using a set of four double-pointed needles, then move on to a circular needle, changing lengths as required. Designed to be worked by an expert knitter who has had experience in knitting in the round, the lace cloth would look attractive laid over a plain cloth in a deep colour which would show off the intricacy of the design. Alternatively, it could be used alone as the centrepiece on a polished wooden dining table.

When all the knitting has been completed, sew in the ends and spend some time pinning out and blocking the cloth to enhance the beauty of the wave-patterned edging.

Materials
Ecru fine cotton yarn
Set of four double-pointed knitting needles and a circular needle, changing lengths as required
Pins

Measurement
The original cloth measures 1 m (39½ in) in diameter.

Abbreviations
Knitting abbreviations appear on page 21. Special abbreviations for this pattern:
yf = yarn forward – note that this abbreviation is also used for yarn round needle

psso = pass slipped stitch over
skpo = sl 1, k1, psso
k1B = knit into back of stitch
inc = increase one stitch

Working the cloth
Using a set of four needles cast on 10 sts (3 sts on each of 2 needles and 4 sts on the 3rd needle).

Join into a circle and work in rounds.

Mark beginning of round with a coloured thread and move this marker as required.

ROUND 1 [Yf, k1] 10 times – 20 sts.
ROUND 2 AND EVERY ALTERNATE ROUND Knit.
ROUND 3 [K1, inc in next st] 10 times – 30 sts.
ROUND 5 [K1, yf, k1, yf, k1] 10 times – 50 sts.
ROUND 7 [K2, yf, k1, yf, k2] 10 times.
ROUND 9 [K3, yf, k1, yf, k3] 10 times.
ROUND 11 [K4, yf, k1, yf, k4] 10 times.
ROUND 13 [K5, yf, k1, yf, k5] 10 times.
ROUND 15 [Yf, k6, yf, k1, yf, k6] 10 times.
ROUND 17 [K1, yf, skpo, k11, k2 tog, yf] 10 times.
ROUND 19 [K1, yf, k1, skpo, k9, k2 tog, k1, yf] 10 times.
ROUND 21 [K1, yf, k2, skpo, k7, k2 tog, k2, yf] 10 times.
ROUND 23 [K1, yf, k3, skpo, k5, k2 tog, k3, yf] 10 times.
ROUND 25 [K1, yf, k4, skpo, k3, k2 tog, k4, yf] 10 times.
ROUND 27 [K1, yf, k5, skpo, k1, k2 tog, k5, yf] 10 times.
ROUND 29 [K1, yf, k6, sl 1, k2 tog, psso, k6, yf] 10 times – 160 sts.
ROUND 31 [K1, yf, k5, k2 tog, yf, k1, yf, skpo, k5, yf] 10 times.
ROUND 33 [K6, k2 tog, k1, yf, k1, yf, k1, skpo, k5] 10 times.
ROUND 35 [K5, k2 tog, k2, yf, k1, yf, k2, skpo, k4] 10 times.
ROUND 37 [K4, k2 tog, k3, yf, k1, yf, k3,

skpo, k3] 10 times.

ROUND 39 [K3, k2 tog, k4, yf, k1, yf, k4, skpo, k2] 10 times.

ROUND 41 [K2, k2 tog, k5, yf, k1, yf, k5, skpo, k1] 10 times.

ROUND 43 [K1, k2 tog, k6, yf, k1, yf, k6, skpo] 10 times.

ROUND 45 Sl last st of last round onto beg of new round then work as follows: [Sl 1, k2 tog, psso, yf, k7, yf, k1, yf, k7, yf] 10 times – 200 sts.

ROUND 47 [K2, yf, k8, yf, k1, yf, k8, yf, k1] 10 times.

ROUND 49 Sl last st of last round onto beg of new round then work as follows: [Sl 1, k2 tog, psso, yf, k1b, yf, skpo, k7, yf, k1, yf, k7, k2 tog, yf, k1B, yf] 10 times.

ROUND 51 [K1B, yf, k3, yf, skpo, k7, yf, k1, yf, k7, k2 tog, yf, k3, yf] 10 times.

ROUND 53 Sl last st of last round onto beg of new round then work as follows: [Sl 1, k2 tog, psso, yf, sl 1, k2 tog, psso, yf, k1B, yf, skpo, k15, k2 tog, yf, k1B, yf, sl 1, k2 tog, psso, yf] 10 times.

ROUND 55 [K3, yf, k1B, yf, k3, yf, skpo, k13, k2 tog, yf, k3, yf, k1B, yf] 10 times.

ROUND 57 [* Yf, sl 1, k2 tog, psso; rep from * 3 times in all, yf, k1B, yf, skpo, k11, k2 tog, yf, k1B, ** yf, sl 1, k2 tog, psso; rep from ** once more] 10 times.

ROUND 59 [K1, yf, k1B, yf, k3, yf, k1B, yf, k3, yf, skpo, k9, k2 tog, yf, k3, yf, k1B, yf, k2] 10 times.

ROUND 61 Sl first st of next round onto end of last round then work as follows: [* Yf, sl 1, k2 tog, psso; rep from * 4 times in all, yf, k1B, yf, skpo, k7, k2 tog, yf, k1B, ** yf, sl 1, k2 tog, psso; rep from ** 3 times in all] 10 times.

ROUND 63 [* K3, yf, k1B, yf; rep from * once more, k3, yf, skpo, k5, k2 tog, yf, ** k3, yf, k1B, yf; rep from ** once more] 10 times.

ROUND 65 [* Yf, sl 1, k2 tog, psso; rep

from * 5 times in all, yf, k1B, yf, skpo, k3, k2 tog, yf, k1B, ** yf, sl 1, k2 tog, psso; rep from ** 4 times in all] 10 times.

ROUND 67 [K1, * yf, k1B, yf, k3; rep from * 3 times in all, yf, skpo, k1, k2 tog, ** yf, k3, yf, k1B; rep from ** once more, yf, k2] 10 times.

ROUND 69 Sl first st of next round onto end of last round then work as follows: [* Yf, sl 1, k2 tog, psso; rep from * 6 times in all, yf, k1B, yf, sl 1, k2 tog, psso, yf, k1B, ** yf, sl 1, k2 tog, psso; rep from ** 5 times in all] 10 times.

ROUND 71 [* K3, yf, k1B, yf; rep from * 7 times in all] 10 times.

ROUND 73 [* Yf, sl 1, k2 tog, psso; rep from * 14 times in all] 10 times.

ROUND 75 [* K1, yf, k1B, yf, K2; rep from * 7 times in all] 10 times.

ROUND 77 Sl first st of next round onto end of last round then work as follows: [* Yf, sl 1, k2 tog, psso; rep from * 14 times in all] 10 times.

ROUND 79 [* K3, yf, k1B, yf; rep from * 7 times in all] 10 times.

ROUND 81 [* Yf, sl 1, k2 tog, psso; rep from * 14 times in all] 10 times.

ROUND 83 [* K1, yf, k1B, yf, k2; rep from * 7 times in all] 10 times.

ROUND 85 Sl first st of next round onto end of last round then work as follows: [* Yf, sl 1, k2 tog, psso; rep from * 14 times in all] 10 times.

ROUND 87 [* K3, yf, k1B, yf; rep from * 7 times in all] 10 times.

Note: pattern is now repeated 5 times in the round.

ROUND 89 [* (Yf, sl 1, k2 tog, psso) 3 times, yf, k3; rep from * 7 times] 5 times.

ROUND 91 [* K1, yf, skpo, k1, k2 tog, yf, k4; rep from * 7 times in all] 5 times.

ROUND 93 [* K2, yf, sl 1, k2 tog, psso, yf, k3, yf, k1, yf, k1; rep from * 7 times in all] 5 times.

ROUND 95 [* K3, yf, k1, yf, k3, k2 tog, yf,

Knitted in the round, this filigree tablecloth displays petals, leaves and a feather and fan border.

k1, yf, skpo; rep from * 7 times] 5 times.

ROUND 97 Sl first st of next round onto end of last round then work as follows: [* K7, k2 tog, k1, yf, k1, yf, k1, skpo; rep from * 7 times in all] 5 times.

ROUND 99 Sl first st of next round onto end of last round then work as follows: [* K5, k2 tog, k2, yf, k1, yf, k2, skpo; rep from * 7 times in all] 5 times.

ROUND 101 Sl first st of next round onto end of last round then work as follows: [* K3, k2 tog, k3, yf, k1, yf, k3, skpo; rep from * 7 times in all] 5 times.

ROUND 103 Sl first st of next round onto end of last round then work as follows: [* K1, k2 tog, k4, yf, k1, yf, k4, skpo; rep from * 7 times in all] 5 times.

ROUND 105 Sl last st of last round onto beg of new round then work as follows: [* Sl 1, k2 tog, psso, yf, k5, yf, k1, yf, k5, yf; rep from * 7 times in all] 5 times.

ROUND 107 [* K2, yf, k6, yf, k1, yf, k6, yf, k1; rep from * 7 times in all] 5 times.

ROUND 109 Sl last st of last round onto beg of new round then work as follows: [* Yf, sl 1, k2 tog, psso, yf, k1B, yf, skpo, k11, k2 tog, yf, k1B; rep from * 7 times in all] 5 times.

ROUND 111 [* K1, yf, k1B, yf, k3, yf, k2 tog, k9, skpo, yf, k2; rep from * 7 times in all] 5 times. (770 sts).

ROUND 113 Sl first st of next round onto end of last round then work as follows: [* (Yf, sl 1, k2 tog, psso) twice, yf, k1B, yf, k2 tog, k7, skpo, yf, k1B, yf, sl 1, k2 tog, psso; rep from * 7 times] 5 times.

ROUND 115 [* Yf, k3, yf, k1B, yf, k3, yf, k2 tog, k5, skpo, yf, k3, yf, k1B; rep from * 7 times in all] 5 times.

ROUND 117 [* K1, sl 1, k2 tog, psso, k3, yf, sl 1, k2 tog, psso, yf, k1B, yf, k2 tog, k3, skpo, yf, k1B, yf, sl 1, k2 tog, psso, yf, k2; rep from * 7 times in all] 5 times.

ROUND 119 [* P3 tog, p2 tog, k1, yf, k1B, yf, k3, yf, k2 tog, k1, skpo, yf, k3, yf, k1B, yf, k1, p2 tog; rep from * 7 times in all] 5 times.

ROUND 121 [K3, (sl 1, k2 tog, psso, yf) twice, k1B, yf, sl 1, k2 tog, psso, yf, k1B, (yf, sl 1, k2 tog, psso) twice, k2; rep from * 7 times in all] 5 times.

ROUND 123 [* K7, (yf, k1) twice, yf, inc 1, (yf, k1) twice, yf, k6; rep from * 7 times in all] 5 times.

ROUND 125 [* (P2 tog) twice, k4, (yf, k1) 4 times, yf, k2 tog, (yf, k1) 4 times, yf, k4, p2 tog, p1; rep from * 7 times in all] 5 times.

ROUND 127 Knit.

ROUND 129 Knit.

ROUND 131 [* (P2 tog) 4 times, (yf, k2 tog) 3 times, yf, k3 tog, (yf, k2 tog) 3 times, yf, (p2 tog) 4 times; rep from * 7 times in all] 5 times.

ROUND 133 Knit.

ROUND 135 Knit.

ROUND 137 [* (P2 tog) 4 times, (yf, k1) 7 times, yf, (p2 tog) 4 times; rep from * 7 times in all] 5 times.

ROUND 139 Knit.

ROUND 141 Knit.

ROUND 143 Work as round 137th.

ROUND 145 Knit.

ROUND 147 Knit.

ROUND 149 Work as round 137th.

ROUND 151 Knit.

ROUND 153 Knit.

ROUND 155 [* P2 tog, p1, p2 tog, p2, (yf, k1) 9 times, yf, p2, p2 tog, p1, p2 tog; rep from * 7 times in all] 5 times.

ROUND 157 Knit.

ROUND 159 Knit.

ROUND 161 [* (P2 tog) 5 times, (yf, k1) 9 times, yf, (p2 tog) 5 times; rep from * 7 times in all] 5 times.

ROUND 163 Knit.

ROUND 165 Knit.

ROUND 167 Work as round 161st.

ROUND 169 Knit.

ROUND 171 Knit.

ROUND 173 [* (P2 tog) twice, p1, (p2 tog)

twice, (yf, k1) 11 times, yf, (p2 tog) twice, p1, (p2 tog) twice; rep from * 7 times in all] 5 times.

ROUND 175 Knit.

ROUND 177 Knit.

ROUND 179 [* (P2 tog) 6 times, (yf, k1) 11 times, yf, (p2 tog) 6 times; rep from * 7 times in all] 5 times.

ROUND 181 Knit.

ROUND 183 Knit.

Using a crochet hook * (pick up 4 sts, yarn around hook through all 4 sts, yarn around hook, through both sts on hook, 11ch) rep from * all around, ss into top of first group. Fasten off.

Finishing the cloth

Working in sections, pin out the cloth to shape following the illustrated instructions given on page 24. Spray with water and allow each section to dry completely before removing the pins.

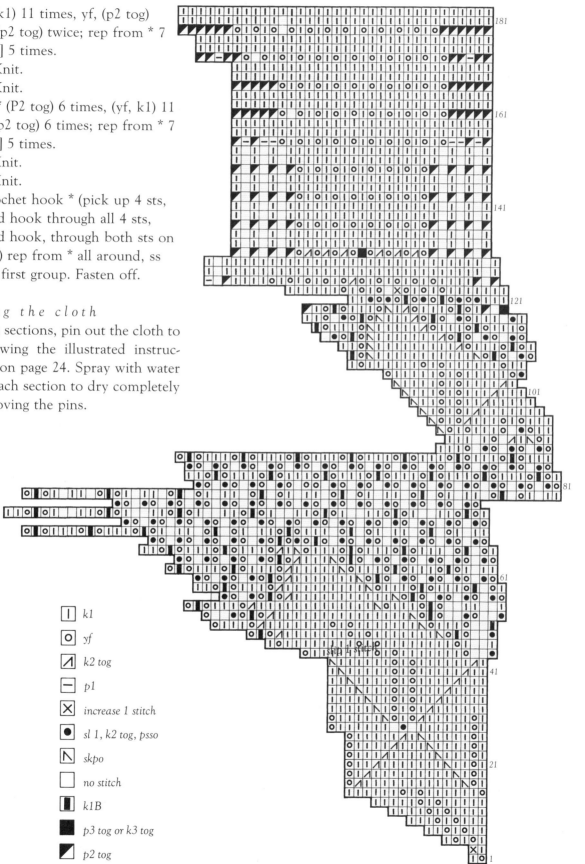

Symbol	Meaning
I	k1
O	yf
◿	k2 tog
−	p1
X	increase 1 stitch
●	sl 1, k2 tog, psso
N	skpo
☐	no stitch
▮	k1B
■	p3 tog or k3 tog
◢	p2 tog

WINDMILL MAT

Octagonal windmill motifs are joined together with two other shapes to make this delicate knitted mat which can be used on a dressing table or as a table centre. A deep edging, knitted separately and attached after all the motifs have been joined, completes the mat. The mat can be made larger or smaller, or the motifs and edging can be worked in heavier cotton to make a cot cover or bedspread.
Suitable for the experienced knitter, this design uses a variety of techniques including circular knitting on a set of double-pointed needles.

Materials
White cotton yarn, no 10 or finer
Pair of 2 mm knitting needles
Set of four 2 mm double-pointed needles
Sewing needle
Pins

Measurements
The mat is made from multiples of three different knitted shapes stitched together, plus a knitted lace edging. You can make the mat larger or smaller by adding or subtracting the relevant shapes.

Abbreviations
Knitting abbreviations appear on page 21. Special abbreviations for this pattern:
yf = yarn forward
skpo = slip 1 stitch, knit 1 stitch, pass slipped stitch over
sk2togpo = slip 1 stitch, knit 2 stitches together, pass slipped stitch over

Working the shapes
SHAPE A (make 6)
Using four needles, cast on 8 sts (3 sts on each of two needles and 2 sts on the third needle).
Join into a circle and work in rounds (page 98).
ROUND 1 Knit.
ROUND 2 * Yf, k1; rep from * to end.
ROUND 3 AND EVERY ALT ROUND Knit.
ROUND 4 * Yf, k2; rep from * to end.
ROUND 6 * Yf, k3; rep from * to end.
ROUND 8 * Yf, k4; rep from * to end.
ROUND 10 * Yf, k5; rep from * to end.
ROUND 12 * Yf, k6; rep from * to end.
ROUND 14 * Yf, k7; rep from * to end.
ROUND 16 * Yf, k8; rep from * to end.
ROUND 18 * Yf, k9; rep from * to end.
ROUND 20 * Yf, k10; rep from * to end.
ROUND 22 * Yf, k11; rep from * to end.
ROUND 24 * Yf, k1, yf, sl 1, k1, psso, k9; rep from * to end.
ROUND 26 * Yf, k1, yf, k2 tog, yf, sl 1, k1, psso, k8; rep from * to end.
ROUND 28 * Yf, k1, yf, [k2 tog, yf] twice, sl 1, k1, psso, k7; rep from * to end.
ROUND 30 * Yf, k1, yf, [k2 tog, yf] 3 times, sl 1 k1, psso, k6; rep from * to end.
ROUND 32 * Yf, k1, yf, [k2 tog, yf] 4 times, sl 1, k1, psso, k5; rep from * to end.
ROUND 34 * Yf, k1, yf, [k2 tog, yf] 5 times, sl 1, k1, psso, k4; rep from * to end.
ROUND 36 * Yf, k1, yf, [k2 tog, yf] 6 times, sl 1, k1, psso, k3; rep from * to end.
ROUND 38 * Yf, k1, yf, [k2 tog, yf] 7 times, sl 1, k1, psso, k2; rep from * to end.
ROUND 40 * Yf, k1, yf, [k2 tog, yf] 8 times, sl 1, k1, psso, k1; rep from * to end.
ROUND 42 * Yf, k1, yf, [k2 tog, yf] 9 times, sl 1, k1, psso; rep from * to end.

A series of windmill motifs makes a delightful and decorative mat for the dining or dressing table. The deep border is knitted separately and joined once the mat has been completed.

ROUND 43 Knit.
Cast off loosely knitwise until there are 22 sts left on the left-hand needle.

LINKING SQUARE
Change to the pair of needles and continue on these 22 sts, working backwards and forwards in rows as follows:
ROW 1 (RIGHT SIDE FACING) Sl 1, k to end.

ROW 2 Sl 1, p to end.
ROW 3 Sl 1, k to end.
Repeat these 3 rows 12 times more.
NEXT ROW Sl 1, k to end.
NEXT ROW Sl 1, p to end.
Cast off loosely knitwise.

SHAPE B (make 6)
Work as for shape A until round 43 is complete. Cast off all sts loosely knitwise.

SHAPE C (make 6)

Using pair of needles, cast on 22 sts.

ROW 1 (RIGHT SIDE FACING) Sl 1, k to end.

ROW 2 Sl 1, p to end.

ROW 3 Sl 1, k to last 2 sts, k2 tog.

Repeat these 3 rows for the pattern, **at the same time**, decrease one st at end of every right side row until 2 sts remain.

NEXT ROW K2 tog and fasten off.

Joining the shapes

1 Sew in the ends. Pin out the shapes following the illustrated instructions on page 24, making sure that all the hexagon, square and triangular shapes are the same size. Spray lightly with water and allow to dry completely.

2 Using the diagram below as a guide, stitch the shapes together using one of the methods shown on page 24. When complete, press the mat lightly.

Working the edging

Cast on 33 sts.

ROW 1 (RIGHT SIDE FACING) Sl 1, k2, yf, k2 tog, yf, K5, yf, sk2togpo, yf, k5, yf, k2 tog, yf, k1, [yf, k2 tog] 5 times, yf, k2.

ROW 2 K14, p17, k2, yf, k2 tog, k1.

ROW 3 Sl 1, k2, yf, k2 tog, yf, k1, k2 tog, p1, skpo, k1, p1, k1, k2 tog, p1, skpo, k1, yf, k2 tog, yf, k2, [yf, k2 tog] 5 times, yf, k2.

ROW 4 K15, p5, [k1, p2] twice, k1, p3, k2, yf, k2 tog, k1.

ROW 5 Sl 1, k2, yf, k2 tog, yf, k1, yf, k2 tog, p1, skpo, p1, k2 tog, p1, skpo, yf, k1, yf, k2 tog, yf, k3, [yf, k2 tog] 5 times, yf, k2.

ROW 6 K16, p6, k1, [p1, k1] twice, p4, k2, yf, k2 tog, k1.

ROW 7 Sl 1, k2, yf, k2 tog, yf, k3, yf, sk2togpo, p1, k3 tog, yf, k3, yf, k2 tog, yf, k4, [yf, k2 tog] 5 times, yf, k2.

ROW 8 K17, p15, k2, yf, k2 tog, k1.

ROW 9 Sl 1, k2, yf, k2 tog, yf, k5, yf, sk2togpo, yf, k5, yf, k2 tog, yf, k5, [yf, k2 tog] 5 times, yf, k2.

ROW 10 K18, p17, k2, yf, k2 tog, k1.

ROW 11 Sl 1, k2, yf, k2 tog, yf, k1, k2 tog, p1, skpo, k1, p1, k1, k2 tog, p1, skpo, k1, yf, k2 tog, yf, k6, [yf, k2 tog] 5 times, yf, k2.

ROW 12 K19, p5, [k1, p2] twice, k1, p3, k2, yf, k2 tog, k1.

ROW 13 Sl 1, k2, yf, k2 tog, yf, k1, yf, k2 tog, p1, skpo, p1, k2 tog, p1, skpo, yf, k1, yf, k2 tog, yf, k7, [yf, k2 tog] 5 times, yf, k2.

ROW 14 K20, p6, k1, [p1, k1] twice, p4, k2, yf, k2 tog, k1.

ROW 15 Sl 1, k2, yf, k2 tog, yf, k3, yf, sk2togpo, p1, k3 tog, yf, k3, yf, k2 tog, yf, k8, [yf, k2 tog] 5 times, yf, k2.

ROW 16 K21, p15, k2, yf, k2 tog, k1.

ROW 17 Sl 1, k2, yf, k2 tog, yf, k5, sk2togpo, yf, k5, yf, k2 tog, yf, k9, [yf, k2 tog] 5 times, yf, k2.

ROW 18 K22, p17, k2, yf, k2 tog, k1.

ROW 19 Sl 1, k2, yf, k2 tog, yf, k1, k2 tog, p1, skpo, k1, p1, k1, k2 tog, p1, skpo, k1, yf, k2 tog, yf, k10, [yf, k2 tog] 5 times, yf, k2.

ROW 20 K23, p5, [k1, p2] twice, k1, p3, k2, yf, k2 tog, k1.

ROW 21 Sl 1, k2, yf, k2 tog, yf, k1, yf, k2 tog, p1, skpo, p1, k2 tog, p1, skpo, yf, k1, yf, k2 tog, yf, k11, [yf, k2 tog] 5 times, yf, k2.

ROW 22 K24, p6, k1, [p1, k1] twice, p4, k2, yf, k2 tog, k1.

ROW 23 Sl 1, k2, yf, k2 tog, yf, k3, yf, sk2togpo, p1, k3 tog, yf, k3, yf, k2 tog, yf, k12, [yf, k2 tog] 5 times, yf, k2.

ROW 24 Cast off 12 sts loosely knitwise, k next 12 sts, p15, k2, yf, k2 tog, k1. (33 sts)

Repeat rows 1 to 24 until the edging is long enough to go round the outer edge of the mat, ending with a 24th row and allowing a little extra edging at each corner so it will lie flat when attached.

Applying the edging

1 Sew in the ends. Pin out the edging following the illustrated instructions given on page 24. Spray lightly with water and allow to dry thoroughly.

2 Pin the edging around the mat making sure you space out the points evenly and that you gather the corners to fit. Oversew the edging in place, taking care not to pull the stitches tight. Carefully sew together the cast-on and cast-off sides of the edging.

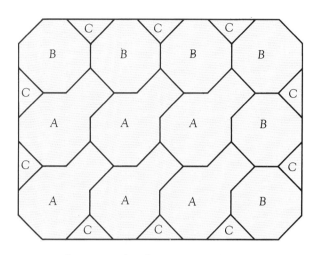

Diagram to show how pieces are stitched together

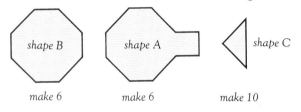

shape B   shape A   shape C

make 6   make 6   make 10

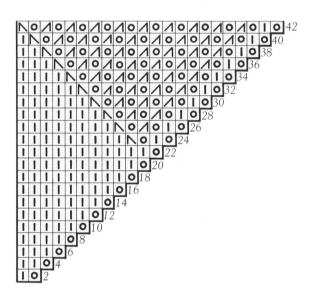

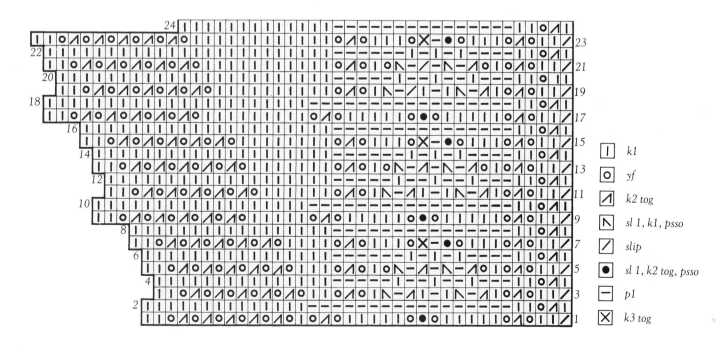

	k1
o	yf
⋀	k2 tog
⋂	sl 1, k1, psso
⁄	slip
●	sl 1, k2 tog, psso
–	p1
✕	k3 tog

SCANDINAVIAN TOWEL

A deep, knitted border complements this cream towel perfectly and it would be easy to decorate all your towels in the same way. Work the same pattern in fine cotton to make narrower edging for face flannels, guest towels and a towelling robe. When working the border, take care to finish the knitting at the end of one complete pattern repeat to make sure that the design at each end of the strip is perfectly symmetrical. Instructions for two more deep border designs are given on page 65.

Materials
Cream double knitting weight cotton
Cream towel
Pair of 3.5 mm knitting needles
Matching sewing thread
Sewing needle
Pins
Starch (optional)

Measurements
Each pattern repeat measures approximately 8 cm (3 in) and seven pattern repeats were needed to edge the hand towel shown here. To edge a larger towel, work further complete pattern repeats until you reach the desired length.

Abbreviations
Knitting abbreviations appear on page 21.

Working the edging
Cast on 16 sts and knit 1 row.
ROW 1 Yo, k2 tog, k1, yo, k10, yo, k2 tog, k1.

ROW 2 K2, yo, k2 tog, k12, p1.
ROW 3 Yo, k2 tog, k1, yo, k2 tog, yo, k9, yo, k2 tog, k1.
ROW 4 K2, yo, k2 tog, k13, p1.
ROW 5 Yo, k2 tog, k1, [yo, k2 tog] twice, yo, k8, yo, k2 tog, k1.
ROW 6 K2, yo, k2 tog, k14, p1.
ROW 7 Yo, k2 tog, k1, [yo, k2 tog] 3 times, yo, k7, yo, k2 tog, k1.
ROW 8 K2, yo, k2 tog, k15, p1.
ROW 9 Yo, k2 tog, k1, [yo, k2 tog] 4 times, yo, k6, yo, k2 tog, k1.
ROW 10 K2, yo, k2 tog, k16, p1.
ROW 11 Yo, k2 tog, k1, [yo, k2 tog] 5 times, yo, k5, yo, k2 tog, k1.
ROW 12 K2, yo, k2 tog, k17, p1.
ROW 13 Yo, k2 tog, k1, [yo, k2 tog] 6 times, yo, k4, yo, k2 tog, k1.
ROW 14 K2, yo, k2 tog, k18, p1.
ROW 15 Yo, k2 tog, k1, [yo, k2 tog] 7 times, yo, k3, yo, k2 tog, k1.
ROW 16 K2, yo, k2 tog, k19, p1.
ROW 17 Yo, [k2 tog] twice, [yo, k2 tog] 7 times, k3, yo, k2 tog, k1.
ROW 18 Rep row 14.
ROW 19 Yo, [k2 tog] twice, [yo, k2 tog] 6 times, k4, yo, k2 tog, k1.
ROW 20 Rep row 12.
ROW 21 Yo, [k2 tog] twice, [yo, k2 tog] 5 times, k5, yo, k2 tog, k1.
ROW 22 Rep row 10.
ROW 23 Yo, [k2 tog] twice, [yo, k2 tog] 4 times, k6, yo, k2 tog, k1.
ROW 24 Rep row 8.
ROW 25 Yo, [k2 tog] twice, [yo, k2 tog] 3 times, k7, yo, k2 tog, k1.
ROW 26 Rep row 6.
ROW 27 Yo, [k2 tog] twice, [yo, k2 tog] twice, k8, yo, k2 tog, k1.
ROW 28 Rep row 4.
ROW 29 Yo, [k2 tog] twice, yo, k2 tog, k9, yo, k2 tog, k1.
ROW 30 Rep row 2.
ROW 31 Yo, [k2 tog] twice, k10, yo, k2 tog, k1.
ROW 32 K2, yo, k2 tog, k11, p1.

Attractive edgings turn plain towels into heirloom pieces perfect for a wedding or anniversary gift. Make a more delicate border for guest towels or face cloths using a finer weight cotton.

Repeat rows 1 to 32 until the edging is the required length, ending with a 32nd row.

Cast off loosely knitwise.

Applying the edging

1 Sew in the ends. Pin out the edging following the illustrated instructions given on page 24. Spray with water and allow to dry completely before removing the pins. For a starched finish, choose a soft-finish starch and apply it following the manufacturer's instruction before pinning out.

2 Pin the edging along one short edge of the towel, making sure you space out the points evenly. Oversew the edging in place with matching sewing thread, taking care not to pull the stitches tight.

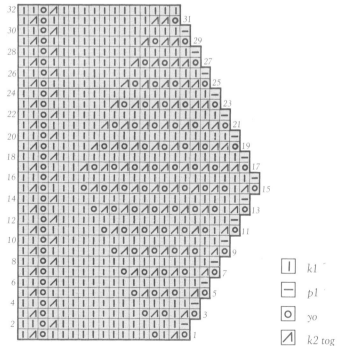

☐	k1
☐	p1
☐	yo
☐	k2 tog

VICTORIAN BEDSPREAD

Knit this Victorian-style bedspread in heavy white cotton yarn and create a wonderful heirloom which can be enjoyed by you and your family for many years to come. The bedspread is knitted in squares and you will need to make four of the following motifs to complete one whole pattern. The motifs are stitched together after pinning out and blocking, then the simple ribbed edging is attached.

When laundering the bedspread, allow it to dry naturally away from sunlight and artificial heat. If necessary, press the bedspread lightly on the wrong side with a warm iron over a well-padded surface, taking care not to crush the raised leaf shapes. Check the seams over periodically to make sure that none of the stitching has worked loose and make repairs as soon as possible.

When storing the bedspread for long periods of time, first make sure that it is perfectly clean and dry, then wrap it in white, acid-free tissue paper and store it in a cool and dry place.

Materials
White cotton yarn approx 3 to 4 ply
Pair of 3.25 mm knitting needles
Tapestry needle
Pins

Measurements
Each square motif measures approximately 15 cm (6 in) on the original bedspread and the complete pattern is made up of four motifs arranged so that four single leaves touch at the centre. The double size bedspread shown here is made from 168 motifs joined in 12 strips of 14 motifs and the edging is knitted in four overlapping sections. Begin by knitting one complete repeat of the pattern, measure the resulting square motif and then calculate how many squares you will need to knit to make a spread the right size to fit your bed.

Abbreviations
Knitting abbreviations appear on page 21.
Special abbreviations for this pattern:
yf = yarn forward
inc = knit into the front and then the back of the next stitch

Working the motif (make 168)
Place a loop on the needle.
Knit into the front, back and then front of this loop – 3 sts made.
Now proceed as follows:
ROW 1 (RIGHT SIDE FACING) K1, [yf, k1] twice.
ROW 2 Inc in first st, p3, inc in last st.
ROW 3 K3, yf, k1, yf, k3.
ROW 4 Inc in first st, k1, p5, k1, inc in last st.
ROW 5 K5, yf, k1, yf, k5.
ROW 6 Inc in first st, k2, p7, k2, inc in last st.
ROW 7 K7, yf, k1, yf, k7.
ROW 8 Inc in first st, k3, p9, k3, inc in last st.

A classic and timeless piece, this beautiful knitted bedspread is made up in squares, four of which form the pattern. The bedspread can be adapted to fit any size bed.

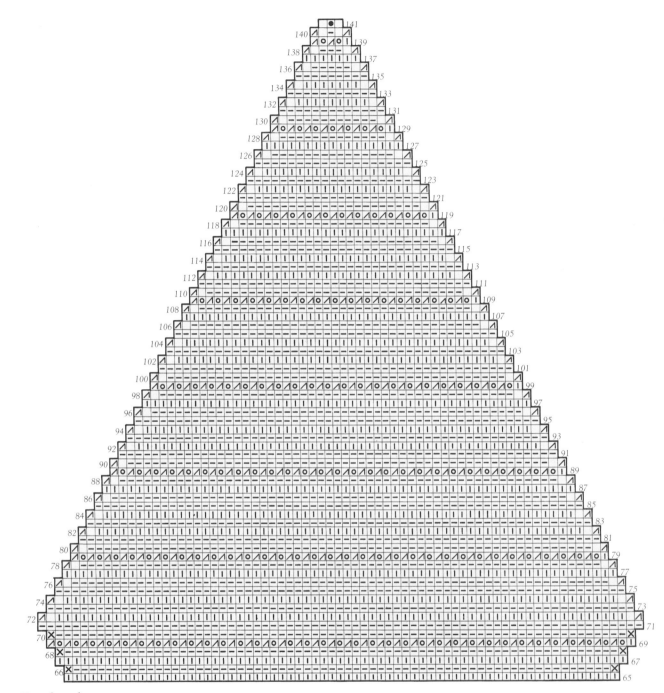

Chart for eyelet pattern

Chart for border

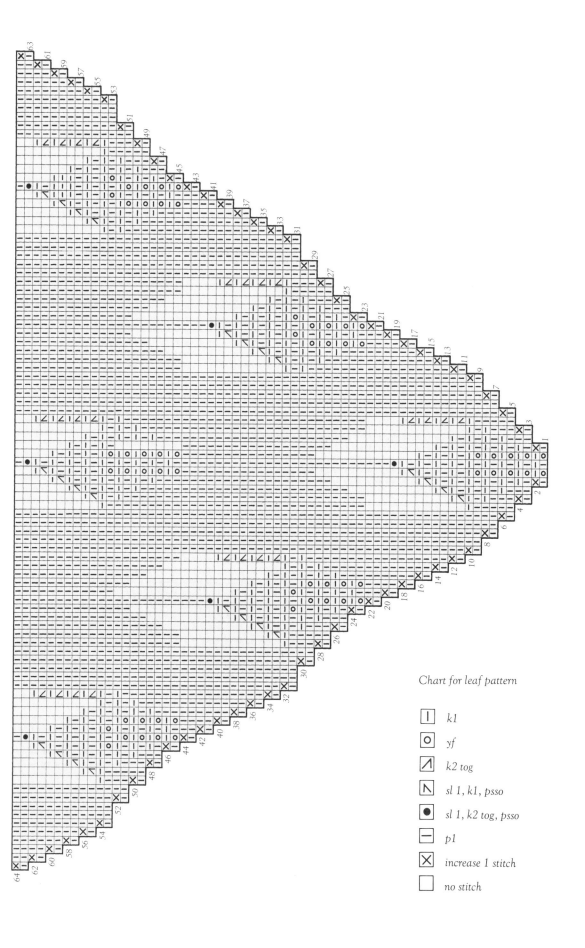

Chart for leaf pattern

$\boxed{	}$	k1
$\boxed{\text{o}}$	yf
$\boxed{/}$	k2 tog
$\boxed{\backslash}$	sl 1, k1, psso
$\boxed{\bullet}$	sl 1, k2 tog, psso
$\boxed{-}$	p1
$\boxed{\times}$	increase 1 stitch
$\boxed{}$	no stitch

ROW 9 K9, yf, k1, yf, k9.

ROW 10 Inc in first st, k4, p11, k4, inc in last st.

ROW 11 K6, sl 1, k1, psso, k7, k2 tog, k6.

ROW 12 Inc in first st, k5, p9, k5, inc in last st.

ROW 13 K7, sl 1, k1, psso, k5, k2 tog, k7.

ROW 14 Inc in first st, k6, p7, k6, inc in last st.

ROW 15 K8, sl 1, k1, psso, k3, k2 tog, k8.

ROW 16 Inc in first st, k7, p5, k7, inc in last st.

ROW 17 K9, sl 1, k1, psso, k1, k2 tog, k9.

ROW 18 Inc in first st, k8, p3, k8, inc in last st.

ROW 19 K10, sl 1, k2 tog, psso, k10.

ROW 20 Inc in first st, k19, inc in last st.

ROW 21 K23.

ROW 22 Inc in first st, k21, inc in last st (25 sts).

ROW 23 [K1, yf] twice, k21, [yf, k1] twice.

ROW 24 Inc in first st, p3, k21, p3, inc in last st.

ROW 25 K3, yf, k1, k23, yf, k1, yf, k3.

ROW 26 Inc in first st, k1, p5, k21, p5, k1, inc in last st.

ROW 27 K5, yf, k1, yf, k25, yf, k1, yf, k5.

ROW 28 Inc in first st, k2, p7, k21, p7, k2, inc in last st.

ROW 29 K7, yf, k1, yf, k27, yf, k1, yf, k7.

ROW 30 Inc in first st, k3, p9, k21, p9, k3, inc in last st.

ROW 31 K9, yf, k1, yf, k29, yf, k1, yf, k9.

ROW 32 Inc in first st, k4, p11, k21, p11, k4, inc in last st.

ROW 33 K6, sl 1, k1, psso, k7, k2 tog, k21, sl 1, k1, psso, k7, k2 tog, k6.

ROW 34 Inc in first st, k5, p9, k21, p9, k5, inc in last st.

ROW 35 K7, sl 1, k1, psso, k5, k2 tog, k21, sl 1, k1, psso, k5, k2 tog, k7.

ROW 36 Inc in first st, k6, p7, k21, p7, k6, inc in last st.

ROW 37 K8, sl 1, k1, psso, k3, k2 tog, k21, sl 1, k1, psso, k3, k2 tog, k8.

ROW 38 Inc in first st, k7, p5, k21, p5, k7, inc in last st.

ROW 39 K9, sl 1, k1, psso, k1, k2 tog, k21, sl 1, k1, psso, k1, k2 tog, k9.

ROW 40 Inc in first st, k8, p3, k21, p3, k8, inc in last st.

ROW 41 K10, sl 1, k2 tog, psso, k21, sl 1, k2 tog, psso, k10.

ROW 42 Inc in first st, k41, inc in last st.

ROW 43 K45.

ROW 44 Inc in first st, k43, inc in last st (47 sts).

ROW 45 K1, [yf, k1, yf, k21] twice, yf, k1, yf, k1.

ROW 46 Inc in first st, [p3, k21] twice, p3, inc in last st.

ROW 47 K3, [yf, k1, yf, k23] twice, yf, k1, yf, k3.

ROW 48 Inc in first st, k1, [p5, k21] twice, p5, k1, inc in last st.

ROW 49 K5, [yf, k1, yf, k25] twice, yf, k1, yf, k5.

ROW 50 Inc in first st, k2, [p7, k21] twice, p7, k2, inc in last st.

ROW 51 K7, [yf, k1, yf, k27] twice, yf, k1, yf, k7.

ROW 52 Inc in first st, k3, [p9, k21] twice, p9, k3, inc in last st.

ROW 53 K9, [yf, k1, yf, k29] twice, yf, k1, yf, k9.

ROW 54 Inc in first st, k4, [p11, k21] twice, p11, k4, inc in last st.

ROW 55 K6, [sl 1, k1, psso, k7, k2 tog, k21] twice, sl 1, k1, psso, k7, k2 tog, k6.

ROW 56 Inc in first st, k5, [p9, k21] twice, p9, k5, inc in last st.

ROW 57 K7, [sl 1, k1, psso, k2 tog, k21] twice, sl 1, k1, psso, k5, k2 tog, k7.

ROW 58 Inc in first st, k6, [p7, k21] twice, p7, k6, inc in last st.

ROW 59 K8, [sl 1, k1, psso, k3, k2 tog, k21] twice, sl 1, k1, psso, k3, k2 tog, k8.

ROW 60 Inc in first st, k7, [p5, k21] twice, p5, k7, inc in last st.

ROW 61 K9, [sl 1, k1, psso, k1, k2 tog, k21] twice, sl 1, k1, psso, k1, k2 tog, k9.

ROW 62 Inc in first st, k8, [p8, k21] twice,

p3, k8, inc in last st.

ROW 63 K10, [sl 1, k2 tog, psso, k21] twice, sl 1, k2 tog, psso, k10.

ROW 64 Inc in first st, k63, inc in last st.

Now begin eyelet pattern:

ROW 65 (RIGHT SIDE FACING) K67.

ROW 66 Inc in first st, p to last st, inc in last st.

ROW 67 Knit.

ROW 68 Inc in first st, p to last st, inc in last st.

ROW 69 K1, [yf, k2 tog] to end.

ROW 70 Inc in first st, p to last st, inc in last st

(73 sts)

**ROW 71 Purl.

ROW 72 K2 tog, k to last 2 sts, k2 tog.

ROW 73 Purl.

ROW 74 K2 tog, k to last 2 sts, k2 tog.

ROW 75 Purl.

ROW 76 K2 tog, p to last 2 sts, k2 tog.

ROW 77 Knit.

ROW 78 K2 tog, p to last 2 sts, k2 tog.

ROW 79 K1, [yf, k2 tog] to end.

ROW 80 K2 tog, p to last 2 sts, k2 tog. **

Rep the 10 rows between ** and ** 6 times more – 3 sts remain.

NEXT ROW S1, k2 tog, psso.

Fasten off.

Working the border

Border for longer edge (make 2):

Cast on 33 sts

ROW 1 (RIGHT SIDE FACING) Purl.

ROW 2 Knit.

ROWS 3 AND 4 Rep rows 1 and 2.

ROWS 5, 6 AND 8 Purl.

ROW 7 Knit.

ROW 9 K2, [yf, k2 tog] to last st, k1.

ROW 10 Purl.

Rep these 10 rows until border, when slightly stretched, fits along one longer edge of the bedspread, ending with a 5th pattern row. Cast off.

Border for shorter edge (make 2):

Work as for longer edge of border, but

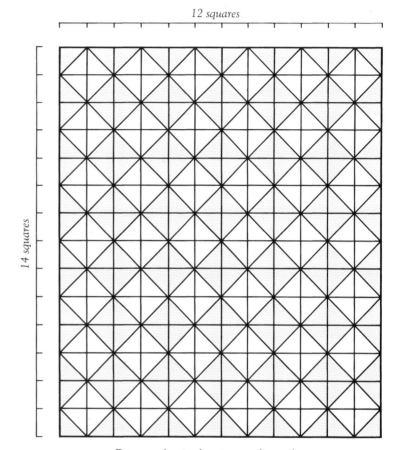

Diagram showing how squares fit together

rep the 10 rows until border, when slightly stretched, fits along one shorter edge of the bedspread, including cast-on and cast-off edges of longer borders, ending with a 5th pattern row.

Cast off.

Making up the bedspread

1 Pin out each motif to the same size, following the illustrated instructions on page 24. Spray with water and allow each motif to dry completely before removing the pins.

2 Stitch the motifs together following the diagram on page 24.

3 Sew the borders in place along the longer edges of the bedspread, then attach the shorter borders.

Pattern Library

LACE EDGINGS

These four edgings can all be worked in heavy, double knitting weight cotton yarn to decorate towels or knitted bedspreads. If you prefer, the three lacy edgings can have a more delicate appearance by simply substituting finer thread and needles.

The designs are knitted vertically and can be stitched to woven fabrics or a piece of knitting.

Abbreviations
Knitting abbreviations appear on page 21.

ZIGZAG EDGING (green)

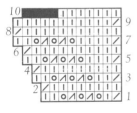

Cast on 8 sts and knit 1 row.
ROW 1 Sl 1, k1, [yo, k2 tog] twice, yo, k2.
ROWS 2, 4, 6 AND 8 Sl 1, knit to end of row.
ROW 3 Sl 1, k2, [yo, k2 tog] twice, yo, k2.
ROW 5 Sl 1, k3, [yo, k2 tog] twice, yo, k2.
ROW 7 Sl 1, k4, [yo, k2 tog] twice, yo, k2.
ROW 9 Sl 1, k11.
ROW 10 Cast off 4 sts, knit to end of row.
Repeat rows 1 to 10.

SAWTOOTH EDGING (peach)

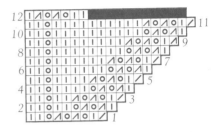

Cast on 8 sts and knit 1 row.
ROW 1 Sl 1, k1, [yo, k2 tog] twice, yo, k2.
ROW 2 K2, yo, k2, [yo, k2 tog] twice, k1.
ROW 3 Sl 1, k1, [yo, k2 tog] twice, k2, yo, k2.
ROW 4 K2, yo, k4, [yo, k2 tog] twice, k1.
ROW 5 Sl 1, k1, [yo, k2 tog] twice, k4, yo, k2.
ROW 6 K2, yo, k6, [yo, k2 tog] twice, k1.
ROW 7 Sl 1, k1, [yo, k2 tog] twice, k6, yo, k2.
ROW 8 K2, yo, k8, [yo, k2 tog] twice, k1.
ROW 9 Sl 1, k1, [yo, k2 tog] twice, k8, yo, k2.
ROW 10 K2, yo, k10, [yo, k2 tog] twice, k1.
ROW 11 Sl 1, k1, [yo, k2 tog] twice, k10, yo, k2.
ROW 12 Cast off 11 sts, k2, [yo, k2 tog] twice, k1.
Repeat rows 1 to 12.

KNIT AND PURL EDGING (blue)

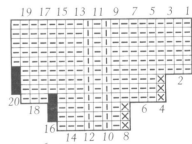

Cast on 6 sts.
ROWS 1, 2 AND 3 Knit.
ROW 4 Cast on 3 sts, knit to end of row.
ROWS 5, 6 AND 7 Knit.
ROW 8 Cast on 3 sts, knit to end of row.
ROWS 9 AND 11 Knit.
ROWS 10 AND 12 Purl.

ROWS 13, 14 AND 15 Knit.

ROW 16 Cast off 3 sts, knit to end of row.

ROWS 17, 18 AND 19 Knit.

ROW 20 Cast off 3 sts, knit to end of row.

Repeat rows 1 to 20.

SCALLOPED TRELLIS EDGING (cream)

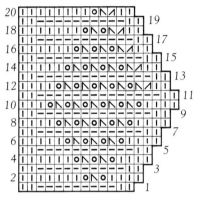

Cast on 13 sts.

ROW 1 AND EVERY ALTERNATE ROW K2, purl to last 2 sts, k2.

ROW 2 K7, yo, sl 1, k1, psso, yo, k4.

ROW 4 K6, [yo, sl 1, k1, psso] twice, yo, k4.

ROW 6 K5, [yo, sl 1, k1, psso] 3 times, yo, k4.

ROW 8 K4, [yo, sl 1, k1, psso] 4 times, yo, k4.

ROW 10 K3, [yo, sl 1, k1, psso] 5 times, yo, k4.

ROW 12 K4, [yo, sl 1, k1, psso] 5 times, k2 tog, k2.

ROW 14 K5, [yo, sl 1, k1, psso] 4 times, k2 tog, k2.

ROW 16 K6, [yo, sl 1, k1, psso] 3 times, k2 tog, k2.

ROW 18 K7, [yo, sl 1, k1, psso] twice, k2 tog, k2.

ROW 20 K8, yo, sl 1, k1, psso, k2 tog, k2.

Repeat rows 1 to 20.

LACE BORDERS

Abbreviations

Knitting abbreviations appear on page 21.

Special abbreviation for Continental:

inc = knit and purl into the next stitch.

Both the designs shown on this page are quite a challenge to knit, but understanding the pattern will become easier once the first complete repeat of each design has been worked. Take special care to work the increase on the Continental border design as described in the Abbreviations section, as a completely different effect is produced if the increase is worked by the more usual method.

DIAMOND AND LACE BORDER (blue)

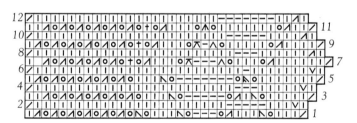

Cast on 34 sts and knit one row.

ROW 1 Sl 1, k3, yo, sl 1, k1, psso, k3, k2 tog, yo, p3, yo, sl 1, k1, psso, k3, yo, sl 1, k1, psso, [yo, k2 tog] 6 times, k1.

ROW 2 Sl 1, k23, p5, k3, [k1, p1] in next st, k1.

ROW 3 Sl 1, k5, yo, sl 1, k1, psso, k1, k2 tog, yo, p5, yo, sl 1, k1, psso, k3, [yo, k2 tog] 6 times, k2.

ROW 4 Sl 1, k24, p3, k5, [k1, p1] in next st, k1.

ROW 5 Sl 1, k7, yo, sl 1, k2 tog, psso, yo, p7, yo, sl 1, k1, psso, k3, [yo, k2 tog] 6 times, k1.

ROW 6 Sl 1, k25, p1, k7, [k1, p1] in next st, k1.

I	k1
∧	k2 tog
+	k1 tbl
N	sl 1, k1, psso
N	sl 1, k2 tog, psso
−	p1
∧	p2 tog
⊼	p2 tog tbl
⋀	p3 tog
V	[k1, p1] in next stitch
X	cast on 1 stitch
■	cast off 1 stitch
O	yo

ROW 7 Sl 1, k6, k2 tog, yo, k3, yo, p2 tog, p3, p2 tog tbl, yo, k3, k2 tog, yo, k1 tbl, [yo, k2 tog] 5 times, k2.

ROW 8 Sl 1, k24, p3, k6, k2 tog, k1.

ROW 9 Sl 1, k4, k2 tog, yo, k5, yo, p2 tog, p1, p2 tog tbl, yo, k3, k2 tog, yo, k1 tbl, [yo, k2 tog] 6 times, k1.

ROW 10 Sl 1, k23, p5, k4, k2 tog, k1.

ROW 11 Sl 1, k2, k2 tog, yo, k7, yo, p3 tog, yo, k3, k2 tog, yo, k1 tbl, [yo, k2 tog] 6 times, k2.

ROW 12 Sl 1, k22, p7, k2, k2 tog, k1.
Repeat rows 1 to 12.

CONTINENTAL BORDER *(peach)*

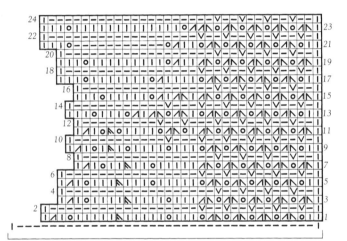

foundation row

I	*k1*
−	*p1*
o	*yo*
⊿	*k2 tog*
⊼	*sl 1, k1, psso*
⋈	*sl 1, k2 tog, psso*
V	*inc*
⋇	*k2 tog tbl*

Cast on 38 sts.

FOUNDATION ROW K1, p36, k1.

ROW 1 K2, [yo, sl 1, k1, psso, k2 tog] 4 times, yo, k3, yo, k5, sl 1, k2 tog, psso, k5, yo, k1, k2 tog, k1.

ROW 2 K1, p18, inc, [p2, inc] 4 times, p1, k1.

ROW 3 K1, [sl 1, k1, psso, k2 tog, yo] 4 times, sl 1, k1, psso, k2 tog, k3, yo, k4, sl 1, k2 tog, psso, k4, yo, k1, k2 tog, k1.

ROW 4 K1, p18, [inc, p2] 4 times, k1.

ROW 5 K2, [yo, sl 1, k1, psso, k2 tog] 4 times, yo, k5, yo, k3, sl 1, k2 tog, psso, k3, yo, k1, k2 tog, k1.

ROW 6 K1, p16, [inc, p2] 4 times, inc, p1, k1.

ROW 7 K1, [sl 1, k1, psso, k2 tog, yo] 4 times, sl 1, k1, psso, k2 tog, k5, yo, k2, sl 1, k2 tog, psso, k2, yo, k1, k2 tog, k1.

ROW 8 K1, p16, [inc, p2] 4 times, k1.

ROW 9 K2, [yo, sl 1, k1, psso, k2 tog] 4 times, yo, k3, yo, k4, yo, k1, sl 1, k2 tog, psso, k1, yo, k1, k2 tog, k1.

ROW 10 K1, p11, inc, p3, [inc, p2] 4 times, inc, p1, k1.

ROW 11 K1, [sl 1, k1, psso, k2 tog, yo] 4 times, sl 1, k1, psso, k2 tog, k1, yo, sl 1, k1, psso, k2 tog, yo, k4, yo, sl 1, k2 tog, psso, yo, k1, k2 tog, k1.

ROW 12 K1, p9, inc, p2, inc, p3, [inc, p2] 4 times, k1.

ROW 13 K2, [yo, sl 1, k1, psso, k2 tog] 4 times, yo, k1, sl 1, k1, psso, k2 tog, yo, sl 1, k1, psso, k2 tog, k1, k2 tog, yo, k3, yo, k3.

ROW 14 Rep row 10.

ROW 15 K1, [sl 1, k1, psso, k2 tog, yo] 4 times, sl 1, k1, psso, k2 tog, k1, sl 1, k1, psso, k2 tog, k1, k2 tog, yo, k5, yo, k3.

ROW 16 Rep row 8.

ROW 17 K2, [yo, sl 1, k1, psso, k2 tog] 4 times, yo, k4, k2 tog, yo, k7, yo, k3.

ROW 18 Rep row 6.

ROW 19 K1, [sl 1, k1, psso, k2 tog, yo] 4 times, sl 1, k1, psso, k2 tog, k2, k2 tog, yo, k9, yo, k3.

ROW 20 Rep row 4.

ROW 21 K2, [yo, sl 1, k1, psso, k2 tog] 4 times, yo, k2, k2 tog, yo, k11, yo, k3.

ROW 22 Rep row 2.

ROW 23 K1, [sl 1, k1, psso, k2 tog, yo] 4 times, sl 1, k1, psso, [k2 tog] twice, yo, k13, yo, k3.

ROW 24 K1, p20, [inc, p2] 4 times, k1.
Repeat rows 1 to 24.

LACE INSERTIONS

Abbreviations
A full list of knitting abbreviations are given on page 21.

Knitted lace insertions are very useful – an insertion can be worked in fine yarn and the resulting lace strip positioned between two pieces of fabric to provide a decorative feature on plain items. An insertion can also serve as an edging or be worked directly into a piece by knitting the pattern repeat in a central panel surrounded by plain panels.

NARROW INSERTION (cream)

Cast on 12 sts.
ROW 1 K3, yo, k2 tog, p2, k1, yo, k2 tog, k2.
ROW 2 K3, yo, k2 tog tbl, k3, yo, k2 tog tbl, k2.
Repeat rows 1 and 2.

ARROW INSERTION (beige)

Cast on 21 sts.
ROW 1 K3, yo, k2 tog, p2, yo, sl 1, k1, psso, k3, k2 tog, yo, p2, k1, yo, k2 tog, k2.
ROWS 2 AND 4 K3, yo, k2 tog tbl, k2, p7, k3, yo, k2 tog tbl, k2.
ROW 3 K3, yo, k2 tog, p2, k1, yo, sl 1, k1, psso, k1, k2 tog, yo, k1, p2, k1, yo,

k2 tog, k2.
ROW 5 K3, yo, k2 tog, p2, k2, yo, sl 1, k2 tog, psso, yo, k2, p2, k1, yo, k2 tog, k2.
ROW 6 K3, yo, k2 tog tbl, k2, p7, k3, yo, k2 tog tbl, k2. Repeat rows 1 to 6.

SINGLE HOLE INSERTION (blue)

Cast on 11 sts.
ROW 1 K2, p2, k1, yo, k2 tog, p2, k2.
ROW 2 K4, p3, k4.
ROW 3 Knit.
ROW 4 K2, p7, k2.
Repeat rows 1 to 4.

LEAF VEIN INSERTION (green)

Cast on 18 sts.
ROW 1 K3, k2 tog, yo, k5, yo, k3, sl 1, k1, psso, k3.
ROW 2 AND EVERY ALTERNATE ROW K3, p12, k3.
ROW 3 K3, k2 tog, k5, yo, k1, yo, k2, sl 1, k1, psso, k3.
ROW 5 K3, k2 tog, k4, yo, k3, yo, k1, sl 1, k1, psso, k3.
ROW 7 K3, k2 tog, k3, yo, k5, yo, sl 1, k1, psso, k3.
ROW 9 K3, k2 tog, k2, yo, k1, yo, k5, sl 1, k1, psso, k3.
ROW 11 K3, k2 tog, k1, yo, k3, yo, k4, sl 1, k1, psso, k3.
ROW 12 K3, p12, k3.
Repeat rows 1 to 12.

LARGE LACE PATTERNS

For the more experienced knitter, the two large lace patterns shown here are rewarding to knit. Work the leaf pattern (green) in fine wool synthetic yarn to make lacy garments, scarves and wraps, or knit several wide strips in heavy cotton and join them together to make an unusual bedspread.

Abbreviations

Knitting abbreviations appear on page 21. Special abbreviation for lace leaves:
inc = knit once into the front and once into the back of the next st.
Abbreviation for cathedral window:
yb = return yarn to back of work before working next stitch.

LACE LEAVES (green)

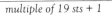

multiple of 19 sts + 1

Cast on a multiple of 19 sts plus 2.
ROWS 1, 3, 5 AND 7 K1, * sl 1, k1, psso, k3, [yo, sl 1, k1, psso] twice, yo, k1, yo, [k2 tog, yo] twice, k3, k2 tog; rep from * to last st, k1.
ROW 2 AND EVERY ALT ROW Purl.

ROW 9 K1, * sl 1, k1, psso, k2, [yo, k2 tog] twice, yo, k3, yo, [sl 1, k1, psso, yo] twice, k2, k2 tog; rep from * to last st, k1.
ROW 11 K1, * sl 1, k1, psso, k1, [yo, k2 tog] twice, yo, k5, yo, [sl 1, k1, psso, yo] twice, k1, k2 tog; rep from * to last st, k1.
ROW 13 K1, * sl 1, k1, psso, [yo, k2 tog] twice, yo, k7, yo, [sl 1, k1, psso, yo] twice, k2 tog; rep from * to last st, inc.
ROW 15 Sl 1, * k1, psso, [yo, k2 tog] twice, yo, k3, k2 tog, k4, yo, [sl 1, k1, psso, yo] twice, sl 1; rep from * to last 2 sts, k1, psso, k1.
ROWS 17, 19, 21 AND 23 K1, * [yo, k2 tog] twice, yo, k3, k2 tog, sl 1, k1, psso, k3, yo [sl 1, k1, psso, yo] twice, k1; rep from * to last st, k1.
ROW 25 K1, * k1, [yo, sl 1, k1, psso] twice, yo, k2, k2 tog, sl 1, k1, psso, k2, [yo, k2 tog] twice, yo, k2; rep from * to last st, k1.
ROW 27 K1, * k2, [yo, sl 1, k1, psso] twice, yo, k1, k2 tog, sl 1, k1, psso, k1, yo, [k2 tog, yo] twice, k3; rep from * to last st, k1.
ROW 29 K1, * k3, [yo, sl 1, k1, psso] twice, yo, k2 tog, sl 1, k1, psso, yo, [k2 tog, yo] twice, k4; rep from * to last st, k1.
ROW 31 K1, * k4, [yo, sl 1, k1, psso] twice, yo, sl 1, k1, psso, yo, [k2 tog, yo] twice, k3, k2 tog; rep from * to last st, k1.
ROW 32 Purl.
Repeat rows 1 to 32.

CATHEDRAL WINDOW LACE (mauve)
Cast on a multiple of 12 sts plus 1.
ROWS 1, 3 AND 5 P1, * yb, sl 1, k1, psso, k3, yo, p1, yo, k3, k2 tog, p1; rep from * to end.
ROWS 2, 4 AND 6 K1, * p5, k1; rep from * to end.
ROW 7 P1, * yo, k3, k2 tog, p1, yb, sl 1, k1, psso, k3, yo, p1; rep from * to end.

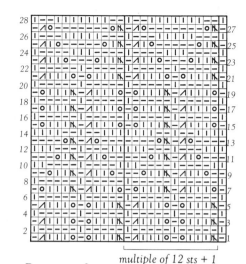

multiple of 12 sts + 1

ROW 8 Rep row 2.

ROW 9 P2, yo, k2, k2 tog, p1, yb, sl 1, k1, psso, k2, * yo, p3, yo, k2, k2 tog, p1, yb, sl 1, k1, psso, k2; rep from * to last 2 sts, yo, p2.

ROW 10 K2, p4, k1, p4, * k3, p4, k1, p4; rep from * to last 2 sts, k2.

ROW 11 P3, yo, k1, k2 tog, p1, yb, sl 1, k1, psso, k1, * yo, p5, yo, k1, k2 tog, p1, yb, sl 1, k1, psso, k1; rep from * to last 3 sts, yo, p3.

ROW 12 K3, p3, k1, p3, * k5, p3, k1, p3; rep from * to last 3 sts, k3.

ROW 13 P4, yo, k2 tog, p1, yb, sl 1, k1, psso, * yo, p7, yo, k2 tog, p1, yb, sl 1, k1, psso; rep from * to last 4 sts, yo, p4.

ROW 14 K4, p2, k1, p2, * k7, p2, k1, p2; rep from * to last 4 sts, k4.

ROWS 15, 17 AND 19 Rep row 7.

ROWS 16, 18 AND 20 Rep row 2.

ROW 21 P1, * yb, sl 1, k1, psso, k3, yo, p1, yo, k3, k2 tog, p1; rep from * to end.

ROW 22 Rep row 2.

ROW 23 P1, * yb, sl 1, k1, psso, k2, yo, p3, yo, k2, k2 tog, p1; rep from * to end.

ROW 24 K1, * p4, k3, p4, k1; rep from * to end.

ROW 25 P1, * yb, sl 1, k1, psso, k1, yo, p5, yo, k1, k2 tog, p1; rep from * to end.

ROW 26 K1, * p3, k5, p3, k1; rep from * to end.

ROW 27 P1, * yb, sl 1, k1, psso, yo, p7, yo, k2 tog, p1; rep from * to end.

ROW 28 K1, * p2, k7, p2, k1; rep from * to end.

Repeat rows 1 to 28.

EYELET PATTERNS

Abbreviations

Knitting abbreviations appear on page 21.

Eyelet patterns are probably the easiest lace design to knit, relying for their effect on simple rows of holes set out in a regular pattern. The blue and beige samples are both worked over a multiple of five stitches and they can be used to make baby clothes and shawls.

⊡	k1
⊟	p1
⊡o	yo
◣	k2 tog
◪	sl 1, k1, psso
◪	yb, sl 1, k1, psso
◪	sl 1, k2 tog, psso
◬	p2 tog

TINY BELLS (beige)

Cast on a multiple of 5 sts.

ROWS 1 AND 3 * K3, p2; rep from * to end.

ROWS 2 AND 4 * K2, p3; rep from * to end.

ROW 5 * Yo, sl 1, k2 tog, psso, yo, p2; rep from * to end.

ROW 6 * K2, p3; rep from * to end.

Repeat rows 1 to 6.

multiple of 5 sts

DAINTY ZIGZAGS (blue)

Cast on a multiple of 5 sts.

ROW 1 * K2, p2 tog, yo, k1; rep from * to end.

ROW 2 AND EVERY ALT ROW Purl.

ROWS 3 AND 7 Knit.

ROW 5 * K3, yo, p2 tog; rep from * to end.

ROW 8 Purl.

Repeat rows 1 to 8.

multiple of 5 sts

CHEVRON EYELETS (cream)

multiple of 9 sts

Cast on a multiple of 9 sts.
ROW 1 * K4, yo, sl 1, k1, psso, k3; rep from * to end.
ROW 2 AND EVERY ALT ROW Purl.
ROW 3 * K2, k2 tog, yo, k1, yo, sl 1, k1, psso, k2; rep from * to end.
ROW 5 * K1, k2 tog, yo, k3, yo, sl 1, k1, psso, k1; rep from * to end.
ROW 7 * K2 tog, yo, k5, yo, sl 1, k1, psso; rep from * to end.
ROW 8 Purl.
Repeat rows 1 to 8.

CHEVRON STRIPES (green)

multiple of 12 sts

multiple of 6 sts + 1

Cast on a multiple of 12 sts.
ROW 1 * K3, yo, sl 1, k1, psso, k2, k2 tog, yo, k1, yo, sl 1, k1, psso; rep from * to end.
ROWS 2 AND 4 Purl.
ROW 3 * K1, k2 tog, yo, k1, yo, sl 1, k1, psso, k1, k2 tog, yo, k1, yo, sl 1, k1, psso; rep from * to end.
ROW 5 * K2 tog, yo, k3, yo, sl 1, k1, psso, k2 tog, yo, k1, yo, sl 1, k1, psso; rep from * to end.
ROW 6 Purl.
Repeat rows 1 to 6.

ALL-OVER PATTERNS

Abbreviations
Knitting abbreviations appear on page 21.

KNOTTED TRELLIS (cream)
Cast on a multiple of 6 sts plus 1.
ROW 1 K1, * yo, p1, p3 tog, p1, yo, k1;

rep from * to end.
ROW 2 AND EVERY ALT ROW Purl.
ROW 3 K2, yo, sl 1, k2 tog, psso, yo, * k3, yo, sl 1, k2 tog, psso, yo; rep from * to last 2 sts, k2.
ROW 5 P2 tog, p1, yo, k1, yo, p1, * p3 tog, p1, yo, k1, yo, p1; rep from * to last 2 sts, p2 tog.
ROW 7 K2 tog, yo, k3, yo, * sl 1, k2 tog, psso, yo, k3, yo; rep from * to last 2 sts, sl 1, k1, psso.
ROW 8 Purl.
Repeat rows 1 to 8.

LACE BLOCKS (mauve)

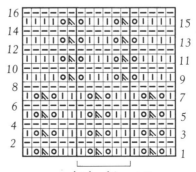

multiple of 6 sts + 5

Like the eyelet patterns, all-over patterns are fairly easy to knit, especially the shell stripes design shown in pink. Try out these patterns using a variety of yarn weights, from fine cotton to heavy, double knitting weight wool, and see what effects are produced.

Cast on a multiple of 6 sts plus 5.

ROWS 1, 3, 5 AND 7 K1, * yo, sl 1, k2 tog, psso, yo, k3; rep from * to last 4 sts, yo, sl 1, k2 tog, psso, yo, k1.

ROW 2 AND EVERY ALT ROW Purl.

ROWS 9, 11, 13 AND 15 K4, * yo, sl 1, k2 tog, psso, yo, k3; rep from * to last st, K1.

ROW 16 Purl.

Repeat rows 1 to 16.

LATTICE LACE (green)

multiple of 4 sts + 1

Cast on a multiple of 4 sts plus 1.

ROW 1 K2, * p1, k3; rep from * to last 3 sts, p1, k2.

ROW 2 P2, * k1, p3; rep from * to last 3 sts, k1, p2.

ROW 3 K2 tog, yo, * p1, yo, k3 tog, yo; rep from * to last 3 sts, p1, yo, k2 tog.

ROWS 4 AND 6 K1, * p3, k1; rep from * to end.

ROW 5 P1, * k3, p1; rep from * to end.

ROW 7 P1, * yo, k3 tog, yo, p1; rep from * to end.

ROW 8 Rep row 2.

Repeat rows 1 to 8.

SHELL STRIPES (pink)

multiple of 7 sts + 1

Cast on a multiple of 7 sts plus 2.

ROW 1 Knit.

ROW 2 Purl.

ROW 3 K2, * yo, p1, p3 tog, p1, yo, k2; rep from * to end.

ROW 4 Purl.

Repeat rows 1 to 4.

CHEVRON AND WAVE PATTERNS

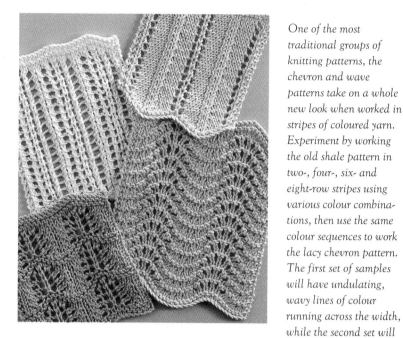

Abbreviations

Knitting abbreviations appear on page 21.

OLD SHALE (pink)

multiple of 18 sts

Cast on a multiple of 18 sts.

ROW 1 Knit.

ROW 2 Purl.

ROW 3 * [K2 tog] 3 times, [yo, k1] 6 times, [k2 tog] 3 times, rep from * to end.

ROW 4 Knit.

Repeat rows 1 to 4.

VANDYKE LACE (cream)

multiple of 9 sts

Cast on a multiple of 9 sts and knit 3 rows before beginning to work pattern.

One of the most traditional groups of knitting patterns, the chevron and wave patterns take on a whole new look when worked in stripes of coloured yarn. Experiment by working the old shale pattern in two-, four-, six- and eight-row stripes using various colour combinations, then use the same colour sequences to work the lacy chevron pattern. The first set of samples will have undulating, wavy lines of colour running across the width, while the second set will show crisp zigzag stripes.

I	*k1*
−	*p1*
⋀	*sl 1, k2 tog, psso*
Λ	*p2 tog*
⋀	*p3 tog*
⟋	*k2 tog*
⟍	*sl 1, k1, psso*
O	*yo*
⋈	*k2 tog tbl*
A	*k3 tog*

ROW 1 * [K2 tog, yo] twice, k1, [yo, k2 tog tbl] twice, rep from * to end.
ROW 2 Purl.
Repeat rows 1 and 2.

LACY CHEVRON (peach)

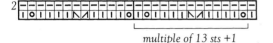

multiple of 13 sts +1

Cast on a multiple of 13 sts plus 1.
ROW 1 * K1, yo, k4, k2 tog, sl 1, k1, psso, k4, yo, rep from * to last st, k1.
ROW 2 Purl.
Repeat rows 1 and 2.

WAVE CREST (fawn)

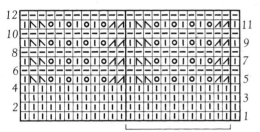

multiple of 12 sts + 1

Cast on a multiple of 12 sts plus 1.
ROW 1 Knit.
ROWS 2, 3 AND 4 Knit.
ROW 5 K1, * [k2 tog] twice, [yo, k1] 3 times, yo, [sl 1, k1, psso] twice, k1, rep from * to end.
ROW 6 Purl.
ROWS 7 TO 12 Rep rows 5 and 6 3 times more.
Repeat rows 1 to 12.

DIAMOND PATTERNS

Abbreviations
Knitting abbreviations appear on page 21.
Special abbreviations for lace diamonds:
p2sso = pass two slipped stitches over.

LACE DIAMONDS (pink)
Cast on a multiple of 6 sts plus 1.
ROW 1 * K1, k2 tog, yo, k1, yo, k2 tog tbl; rep from * to last st, k1.
ROW 2 AND EVERY ALT ROW Purl.
ROW 3 K2 tog, * yo, k3, yo, [sl 1] twice, k1, p2sso; rep from * to last 5 sts, yo, k3, yo, k2 tog tbl.
ROW 5 * K1, yo, k2 tog tbl, k1, k2 tog, yo; rep from * to last st, k1.
ROW 7 K2, * yo, [sl 1] twice, k1, p2sso, yo, k3; rep from * to last 5 sts, yo, [sl 1] twice, k1, p2sso, yo, k2.
ROW 8 Purl.
Repeat rows 1 to 8.

LEAFY DIAMONDS (green)

Diamond patterns are very popular and the samples here demonstrate three different treatments of the same theme. The leafy diamonds (shown in green) is an arrangement of diamond-shaped leaves and could be substituted in the Evening Wrap (page 30). In the blue example, the diamond pattern is enhanced by rows of garter stitch, while the lace diamonds pattern (pink) is quick and easy to knit.

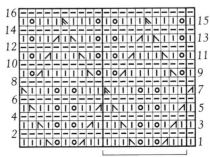

multiple of 10 sts + 1

multiple of 6 sts + 1

Cast on a multiple of 10 sts plus 1.

ROW 1 K3, * k2 tog, yo, k1, yo, sl 1, k1, psso, k5; rep from * to last 8 sts, k2 tog, yo, k1, yo, sl 1, k1, psso, k3.

ROW 2 AND EVERY ALT ROW Purl.

ROW 3 K2, * k2 tog, [k1, yo] twice, k1, sl 1, k1, psso, k3; rep from * to last 9 sts, k2 tog, [k1, yo] twice, k1, sl 1, k1, psso, k2.

ROW 5 K1, * k2 tog, k2, yo, k1, yo, k2, sl 1, k1, psso, k1; rep from * to end.

ROW 7 K2 tog, * k3, yo, k1, yo, k3, sl 1, k2 tog, psso; rep from * to last 9 sts, k3, yo, k1, yo, k3, sl 1, k1, psso.

ROW 9 K1, * yo, sl 1, k1, psso, k5, k2 tog, yo, k1; rep from * to end.

ROW 11 K1, * yo, k1, sl 1, k1, psso, k3, k2 tog, k1, yo, k1; rep from * to end.

ROW 13 K1, * yo, k2, sl 1, k1, psso, k1, k2 tog, k2, yo, k1; rep from * to end.

ROW 15 K1, * yo, k3, sl 1, k2 tog, psso, k3, yo, k1; rep from * to end.

ROW 16 Purl.

Repeat rows 1 to 16.

RIDGED DIAMONDS (blue)

multiple of 10 sts + 3

Cast on a multiple of 10 sts plus 3.

ROW 1 K2, yo, sl 1, k1, psso, k5, k2 tog, yo, * k1, yo, sl 1, k1, psso, k5, k2 tog, yo; rep from * to last 2 sts, k2.

ROW 2 P4, k5, * p5, k5; rep from * to last 4 sts, p4.

ROW 3 K3, * yo, sl 1, k1, psso, k3, k2 tog, yo, k3; rep from * to end.

ROW 4 P5, k3, * p7, k3; rep from * to last 5 sts, p5.

ROW 5 K4, yo, sl 1, k1, psso, k1, k2 tog, yo, * k5, yo, sl 1, k1, psso, k1, k2 tog, yo; rep from * to last 4 sts, k4.

ROW 6 P6, k1, * p9, k1; rep from * to last 6 sts, p6.

ROW 7 K5, yo, sl 1, k2 tog, psso, yo, * k7, yo, sl 1, k2 tog, psso, yo; rep from * to last 5 sts, k5.

ROW 8 Purl.

ROW 9 K4, k2 tog, yo, k1, yo, sl 1, k1, psso, * k5, k2 tog, yo, k1, yo, sl 1, k1, psso; rep from * to last 4 sts, k4.

ROW 10 K4, p5, * k5, p5; rep from * to last 4 sts, k4.

ROW 11 K3, * k2 tog, yo, k3, yo, sl 1, k1, psso, k3; rep from * to end.

ROW 12 K3, * p7, k3; rep from * to end.

ROW 13 K2, k2 tog, yo, k5, yo, sl 1, k1, psso, * k1, k2 tog, yo, k5, yo, sl 1, k1, psso; rep from * to last 2 sts, k2.

ROW 14 P1, k1, * p9, k1; rep from * to last st, p1.

ROW 15 K1, k2 tog, yo, k7, * yo, sl 1, k2 tog, psso, yo, k7; rep from * to last 3 sts, yo, sl 1, k1, psso, k1.

ROW 16 Purl.

Repeat rows 1 to 16.

LACE AND TEXTURES

Lacy knitting contrasts with textured areas formed by working rows of either reverse stocking stitch or garter stitch. Best worked in a fairly substantial yarn to accentuate the textures, the patterns shown produce an interesting surface. Use the patterns to make garments and small household articles such as cushion covers.

Abbreviations
Knitting abbreviations appear on page 21.

I	k1
—	p1
O	yo
◿	k2 tog
◺	p2 tog
N	sl 1, k1, psso
◣	sl1, k2 tog, psso
V	inc
■	cast off 1 stitch
⧄	yo twice

INTERLACED CHEVRONS (peach)

multiple of 16 sts

Cast on a multiple of 16 sts.

ROW 1 Knit.

ROW 2 * K4, p8, k4; rep from * to end.

ROW 3 * P3, k2 tog, k3, yo twice, k3, sl 1, k1, psso, p3; rep from * to end.

ROW 4 * K3, p4, purl into front and back of double yo made on previous row, p4, k3; rep from * to end.

ROW 5 * P2, k2 tog, k3, yo, k2, yo, k3, sl 1, k1, psso, p2; rep from * to end.

ROW 6 * K2, p12, k2; rep from * to end.

ROW 7 * P1, k2 tog, k3, yo, k4, yo, k3, sl 1, k1, psso, p1; rep from * to end.

ROW 8 * K1, p14, k1; rep from * to end.

ROW 9 * K2 tog, k3, yo, k6, yo, k3, sl 1, k1, psso; rep from * to end.

ROW 10 Purl.

Repeat rows 1 to 10.

EGYPTIAN EYELETS (blue)

multiple of 12 sts + 3

Cast on a multiple of 12 sts plus 3.

ROW 1 P2, k11, * p1, k11; rep from * to last 2 sts, p2.

ROW 2 K2, p11, * k1, p11; rep from * to last 2 sts, k2.

ROW 3 * P3, k2, [yo, sl 1, k1, psso] 3 times, k1; rep from * to last 3 sts, p3.

ROW 4 K3, * p9, k3; rep from * to end.

ROW 5 P4, k2, [yo, sl 1, k1, psso] twice, k1, * p5, k2, [yo, sl 1, k1, psso] twice, k1; rep from * to last 4 sts, p4.

ROW 6 K4, p7, * k5, p7; rep from * to last 4 sts, k4.

ROW 7 P5, k2, yo, sl 1, k1, psso, k1, * p7, k2, yo, sl 1, k1, psso, k1; rep from * to last 5 sts, p5.

ROW 8 K5, p5, * k7, p5; rep from * to last 5 sts, k5.

ROW 9 P6, k3, * p9, k3; rep from * to last 6 sts, p6.

ROW 10 K6, p3, * k9, p3; rep from * to last 6 sts, k6.

ROW 11 P7, k1, * p11, k1; rep from * to last 7 sts, p7.

ROW 12 K7, p1, * k11, p1; rep from * to last 7 sts, k7.

ROW 13 Rep row 12.

ROW 14 Rep row 11.

ROW 15 K1, [yo, sl 1, k1, psso] twice, k1, p3, * k2, [yo, sl 1, k1, psso] 3 times, k1, p3; rep from * to last 6 sts, k2, yo, sl 1, k1, psso, k2.

ROW 16 Rep row 9.

ROW 17 K2, yo, sl 1, k1, psso, k1, p5, * k2, [yo, sl 1, k1, psso] twice, k1, p5; rep from * to last 5 sts, k2, yo, sl 1, k1, psso, k1.

ROW 18 P5, k5, * p7, k5; rep from * to last 5 sts, p5.

ROW 19 K1, yo, sl 1, k1, psso, k1, p7, * k2, yo, sl 1, k1, psso, k1, p7; rep from * to last 4 sts, k2, yo, sl 1, k1, psso.

ROW 20 P4, k7, * p5, k7; rep from * to last 4 sts, p4.

ROW 21 Rep row 4.

ROW 22 P3, * k9, p3; rep from * to end.

ROW 23 Rep row 2.

ROW 24 Rep row 1.

Repeat rows 1 to 24.

GARTER STITCH CHECKS (beige)

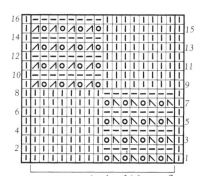

multiple of 16 sts + 2

Cast on a multiple of 16 sts plus 2.

ROWS 1, 3, 5 AND 7 K1, * [sl 1, k1, psso, yo] 4 times, k8; rep from * to last st, k1.

ROWS 2, 4, 6 AND 8 K1, * k8, p8; rep from * to last st, k1.

ROWS 9, 11, 13 AND 15 K1, * k8, [yo, k2 tog] 4 times; rep from * to last st, k1.

ROWS 10, 12, 14 AND 16 K1, * p8, k8; rep from * to last st, k1.

Repeat rows 1 to 16.

RAISED LEAF PATTERNS

Knit four of the triangular raised leaf motifs (cream), arrange them so that the four single leaves touch in the centre, then stitch them together to make a large square. Back the square with matching fabric, or a plain piece of knitting, for use as a cushion cover, or you could work more motifs and stitch the squares together to make a bedspread in the same way as the Victorian bedspread on page 58.

A b b r e v i a t i o n s

Knitting abbreviations appear on page 21. Special abbreviation for leaf motif and shaped leaf edging:

inc = knit once into the front and once into the back of the next stitch.

SHAPED LEAF EDGING (green)

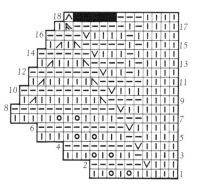

Cast on 8 sts.

ROW 1 K5, yo, k1, yo, k2.

ROW 2 P6, inc in next st, k3.

ROW 3 K4, p1, k2, yo, k1, yo, k3.

ROW 4 P8, inc in next st, k4.

ROW 5 K4, p2, k3, yo, k1, yo, k4.

ROW 6 P10, inc in next st, k5.

ROW 7 K4, p3, k4, yo, k1, yo, k5.

ROW 8 P12, inc in next st, k6.

ROW 9 K4, p4, sl 1, k1, psso, k7, k2 tog, k1.

ROW 10 P10, inc in next st, k7.

ROW 11 K4, p5, sl 1, k1, psso, k5, k2 tog, k1.

ROW 12 P8, inc in next st, k2, p1, k5.

ROW 13 K4, p1, k1, p4, sl 1, k1, psso, k3, k2 tog, k1.

ROW 14 P6, inc in next st, k3, p1, k5.

ROW 15 K4, p1, k1, p5, sl 1, k1, psso, k1, k2 tog, k1.

ROW 16 P4, inc in next st, k4, p1, k5.

ROW 17 K4, p1, k1, p6, sl 1, k2 tog, psso, k1.

ROW 18 P2 tog, cast off next 5 sts using p2 tog st when casting off first st, p3, k4.

Repeat rows 1 to 18.

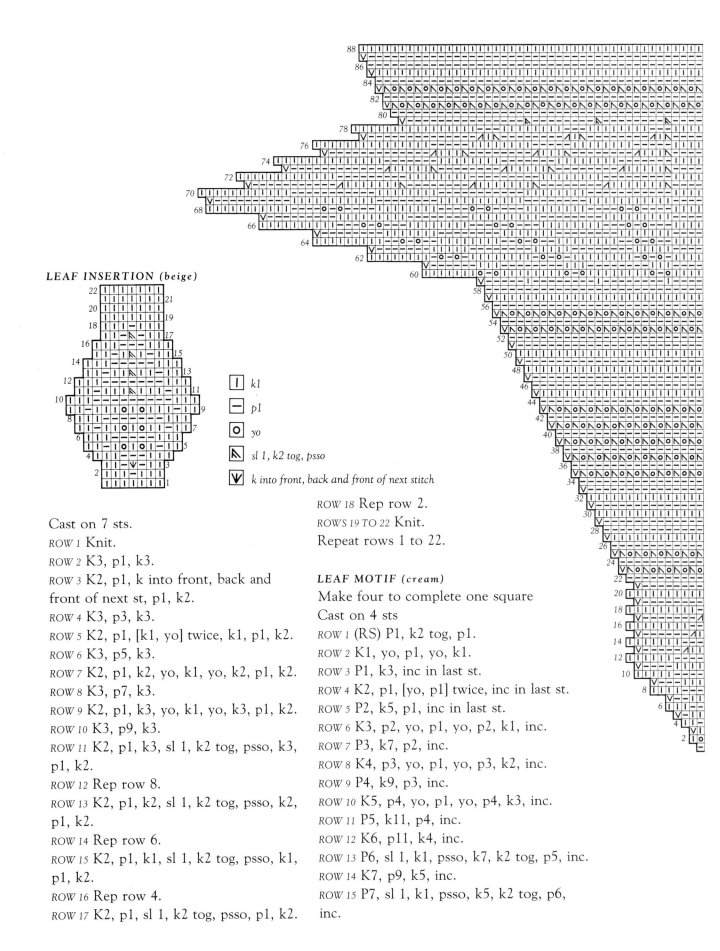

LEAF INSERTION (beige)

☐ I = k1

☐ − = p1

☐ O = yo

☐ ◪ = sl 1, k2 tog, psso

☐ Ⅴ = k into front, back and front of next stitch

Cast on 7 sts.
ROW 1 Knit.
ROW 2 K3, p1, k3.
ROW 3 K2, p1, k into front, back and front of next st, p1, k2.
ROW 4 K3, p3, k3.
ROW 5 K2, p1, [k1, yo] twice, k1, p1, k2.
ROW 6 K3, p5, k3.
ROW 7 K2, p1, k2, yo, k1, yo, k2, p1, k2.
ROW 8 K3, p7, k3.
ROW 9 K2, p1, k3, yo, k1, yo, k3, p1, k2.
ROW 10 K3, p9, k3.
ROW 11 K2, p1, k3, sl 1, k2 tog, psso, k3, p1, k2.
ROW 12 Rep row 8.
ROW 13 K2, p1, k2, sl 1, k2 tog, psso, k2, p1, k2.
ROW 14 Rep row 6.
ROW 15 K2, p1, k1, sl 1, k2 tog, psso, k1, p1, k2.
ROW 16 Rep row 4.
ROW 17 K2, p1, sl 1, k2 tog, psso, p1, k2.

ROW 18 Rep row 2.
ROWS 19 TO 22 Knit.
Repeat rows 1 to 22.

LEAF MOTIF (cream)
Make four to complete one square
Cast on 4 sts
ROW 1 (RS) P1, k2 tog, p1.
ROW 2 K1, yo, p1, yo, k1.
ROW 3 P1, k3, inc in last st.
ROW 4 K2, p1, [yo, p1] twice, inc in last st.
ROW 5 P2, k5, p1, inc in last st.
ROW 6 K3, p2, yo, p1, yo, p2, k1, inc.
ROW 7 P3, k7, p2, inc.
ROW 8 K4, p3, yo, p1, yo, p3, k2, inc.
ROW 9 P4, k9, p3, inc.
ROW 10 K5, p4, yo, p1, yo, p4, k3, inc.
ROW 11 P5, k11, p4, inc.
ROW 12 K6, p11, k4, inc.
ROW 13 P6, sl 1, k1, psso, k7, k2 tog, p5, inc.
ROW 14 K7, p9, k5, inc.
ROW 15 P7, sl 1, k1, psso, k5, k2 tog, p6, inc.

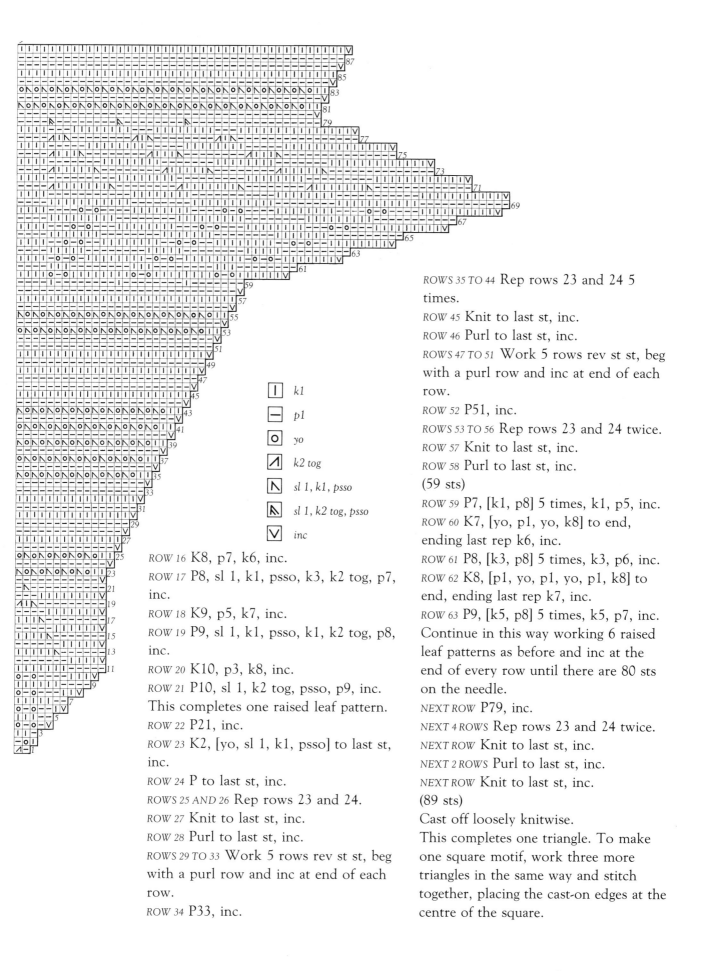

	k1
−	p1
o	yo
⟋	k2 tog
N	sl 1, k1, psso
Ŋ	sl 1, k2 tog, psso
V	inc

ROW 16 K8, p7, k6, inc.

ROW 17 P8, sl 1, k1, psso, k3, k2 tog, p7, inc.

ROW 18 K9, p5, k7, inc.

ROW 19 P9, sl 1, k1, psso, k1, k2 tog, p8, inc.

ROW 20 K10, p3, k8, inc.

ROW 21 P10, sl 1, k2 tog, psso, p9, inc. This completes one raised leaf pattern.

ROW 22 P21, inc.

ROW 23 K2, [yo, sl 1, k1, psso] to last st, inc.

ROW 24 P to last st, inc.

ROWS 25 AND 26 Rep rows 23 and 24.

ROW 27 Knit to last st, inc.

ROW 28 Purl to last st, inc.

ROWS 29 TO 33 Work 5 rows rev st st, beg with a purl row and inc at end of each row.

ROW 34 P33, inc.

ROWS 35 TO 44 Rep rows 23 and 24 5 times.

ROW 45 Knit to last st, inc.

ROW 46 Purl to last st, inc.

ROWS 47 TO 51 Work 5 rows rev st st, beg with a purl row and inc at end of each row.

ROW 52 P51, inc.

ROWS 53 TO 56 Rep rows 23 and 24 twice.

ROW 57 Knit to last st, inc.

ROW 58 Purl to last st, inc. (59 sts)

ROW 59 P7, [k1, p8] 5 times, k1, p5, inc.

ROW 60 K7, [yo, p1, yo, k8] to end, ending last rep k6, inc.

ROW 61 P8, [k3, p8] 5 times, k3, p6, inc.

ROW 62 K8, [p1, yo, p1, yo, p1, k8] to end, ending last rep k7, inc.

ROW 63 P9, [k5, p8] 5 times, k5, p7, inc. Continue in this way working 6 raised leaf patterns as before and inc at the end of every row until there are 80 sts on the needle.

NEXT ROW P79, inc.

NEXT 4 ROWS Rep rows 23 and 24 twice.

NEXT ROW Knit to last st, inc.

NEXT 2 ROWS Purl to last st, inc.

NEXT ROW Knit to last st, inc. (89 sts)

Cast off loosely knitwise.

This completes one triangle. To make one square motif, work three more triangles in the same way and stitch together, placing the cast-on edges at the centre of the square.

USEFUL SUPPLIERS

UNITED KINGDOM

MAIL ORDER
Framecraft
372–376 Summer Lane
Hockley
Birmingham
B19 3QA

Hollyoak Mail Order Supplies
Cogshall Lane
Comberbach
Cheshire
CW9 6BS
*(equipment, pattern books and
yarns)*

The Readicut Wool Co
Terry Mills
Ossett
West Yorkshire
WF5 9SA
(equipment, accessories and yarns)

William Hall (Monsall) Ltd
177 Stanley Road
Cheadle Hulme
Cheshire
SK8 6RF
*(natural and dyed yarns, including
linen and cotton)*

Texere Yarns
College Mill
Barkerend Road
Bradford
West Yorkshire
BD3 9AQ
*(natural silk and cotton yarns, dyed
silk, cotton and wool yarns)*

Jamieson and Smith
90 North Road
Lerwick
ZE1 0PQ
Shetland Isles
(Shetland wool yarn)

MANUFACTURERS
Jaeger Handknitting
McMullen Road
Darlington
Durham
DL1 1YH
(cotton and wool yarns)

Rowan Yarns
Green Lane Mill
Washpit
Holmfirth
West Yorkshire
HD7 1RW
(cotton and wool yarns)

HG Twilley Ltd
Roman Mills
Stamford
Lincolnshire
PE9 1BG
(cotton yarn)

Coats Leisure Crafts Group
39 Durham Street
Kinning Park
Glasgow
G41 1BS
(cotton and wool yarns)

DMC Creative World
Pullman Road
Wigston
Leicester
LE8 2DY
(cotton)

SHOPS
Creativity
45 New Oxford Street
London WC1
(equipment, yarns, patterns)

John Lewis
Oxford Street
London W1A 1EX
(equipment, yarns, patterns)

AUSTRALIA
Box Hill Wool Shop
922 Whitehorse Road
Box Hill
Victoria 3128

Champion Textiles
16–18 O'Connell Street
Newton
New South Wales 2042

Elizabeth's Spinning Wheel
Shop 5 Village Fair
97 Flockton Street
McDowall
Queensland 4053

Fremantle Wool Shed
Shop 9 Manning Arcade
Fremantle
Western Australia 6160

Knitting Nook
17 Adelaide Arcade
Adelaide SA 5000

NEW ZEALAND
Bernina Sewing Centre
St. Lukes Square
Mt Albert
(Branches throughout New
Zealand)

Elna Sewing Centres
City Strand Arcade
Queen Street
Auckland
(Branches throughout New
Zealand)

Masco Ltd The Wool Shop
229 Karangahape Road
Newton
(Branches throughout New
Zealand and Auckland)

GLOSSARY

Ball band – the paper strip around a ball of yarn giving weight, colour and dye lot numbers, fibre content, care instructions.

Blocking – setting the pattern by stretching and pinning out a piece of damp knitting and allowing it to dry.

Border – a *deep* strip of patterned knitting with one straight and one shaped edge. Usually worked in short rows across the width.

Cast off – the last row of knitting worked to form an edge which does not unravel.

Cast on – the first row of knitting stitches which are looped on to the needle and make an edge which does not unravel.

Chart – pattern expressed as symbols.

Decrease – to reduce the number of working stitches on the needle.

Dye lot – the batch of dye used for a specific ball of yarn. Shades can vary between batches, so use yarn from the same batch to make one item.

Edging – a *narrow* strip of patterned knitting with one straight and one shaped edge. Usually worked in short rows across the width.

Garter stitch – knitted fabric in which every row is knitted.

Increase – to make the number of working stitches on the needle.

Insertion – a strip of patterned knitting with parallel edges. Usually worked in short rows across the width.

Knitting pattern – complete instructions showing how to make a knitted article.

Knit – one of the two basic knitting stitches; the other is purl.

Mercerizing – process for cotton which produces a strong, lustrous finish.

Motif – a shaped piece of knitting worked in rounds which can be joined together to make a larger piece.

Pattern repeat – specific number of rows needed to complete one stitch pattern.

Ply – the number of strands which are twisted together to make a yarn.

Purl – one of the two basic knitting stitches; the other is knit.

Shetland shawl – light, lacy shawl knitted in very fine Shetland yarn. Consists of a central panel bordered by four identical, shaped knitted strips.

Slip – to move a stitch from one needle to the other without working it.

Starch – a natural or synthetic substance used for stiffening lace items.

Stitch pattern – ,a sequence of stitches needed to create a specific design, expressed as row-by-row (or round-by-round) instructions, either written or charted.

Stocking stitch – alternate rows of knit and purl.

Tapestry needle – a blunt embroidery needle with a long, large eye.

Tension – the looseness or tightness of a knitted fabric generally expressed as a specific number of rows and stitches in a given area, usually 10 cm (4 in) square.

BIBLIOGRAPHY

Compton, Rae, *The Illustrated Dictionary of Knitting*, Batsford, 1988

Get Knitting, Marshall Cavendish, 1985–1986

Kinzel, M., *First Book of Modern Lace Knitting*, Dover, 1972

Kinzel, M., *Second Book of Modern Lace Knitting*, Dover, 1972

Patons Woolcraft, 25th Edition, Paton & Baldwins, 1989

Rutt, Richard, *A History of Hand Knitting*, Batsford, 1987

Stanley Montse, *The Handknitter's Handbook, 3rd Edition*, David & Charles, 1993

Knitting Index